My Beautiful Mess
-

By Peta Sitcheff

Contents

Chapter 1	**Panic**	13
Chapter 2	**Her**	25
Chapter 3	**Feeling**	31
Chapter 4	**T-Junctions**	41
Chapter 5	**64 614**	47
Chapter 6	**No**	57
Chapter 7	**Humanism**	67
Chapter 8	**Choice**	75
Chapter 9	**Managing the Beast**	89
Chapter 10	**Boundaries**	97
Chapter 11	**Grief**	109
Chapter 12	**Single Life**	121
Chapter 13	**Fear**	125
Chapter 14	**Ego**	133
Chapter 15	**The Spine Girl**	139

Chapter 16	**Outliers**	**145**
Chapter 17	**Niggles**	**149**
Chapter 18	**Disconnection**	**155**
Chapter 19	**Tipping Point**	**159**
Chapter 20	**The Gap**	**165**
Chapter 21	**False Start**	**173**
Chapter 22	**Back to Bite**	**177**
Chapter 23	**Nice to Meet You**	**181**
Chapter 24	**Books**	**189**
Chapter 25	**Truth Bomb**	**197**
Chapter 26	**Today's Wonder**	**203**
Chapter 27	**Lewis**	**215**
Chapter 28	**Joy**	**225**
Chapter 29	**Boggle Brain**	**233**
Chapter 30	**My Birds**	**239**
Chapter 31	**Success**	**243**
Chapter 32	**Good Night Irene**	**251**

"It's all messy.
The hair.
The bed.
The words.
The heart.
Life"

William Leal

"One day you will tell your story of how you've overcome what you are going through, and it will become another person's survival guide."

Anon

Disclaimer

Copyright © 2020 Peta Sitcheff

This work is copyright. Apart from any use as permitted under the Copyright Act 1968, no part may be reproduced, copied, scanned, stored in a retrieval system, recorded or transmitted, in any form or by any means, without the prior written permission of the author or publisher.

ISBN 9780646841229

Editor - Vanessa Barrington (The Right Remark)
www.therightremark.com
Cover design © 2020 Hannah Sutton Design
www.hannahsuttondesign.com
Front cover background photograph by Kensuke Saito surf photography & back cover images courtesy Austrian National Library, Zach Kadolph (sourced from Unsplash)
Author photograph by Prue Aja www.prueaja.com

4 Things to Note About This Book

1.   These pages are a playbook of my last 20 years. A teaching memoir jam packed with lessons illustrated through my own lived experiences. Each particular experience reflects my recollection of events, and opinion at the time. Some events have been compressed or dramatised for the sake of the narrative.

2.   There are a number of characters throughout the script. Each have been generalised, deidentified or had names changed to protect the individuals who inspired the narrative.

3.   I'm not a medical professional, nor am I a psychologist. I'm someone who's lived a little, stuffed up a lot and hopes to offer the wisdom to prevent another from making the same mistakes.

4.   The past few years, I've adopted the discipline of reading one book a week. At the end of each chapter, I've included my references and a few recommended titles that helped me through that particular point in time and thought they might help you too. I now capture these each week via Instagram @petasitcheff

Feel free to join me and become a bookworm too!

From me to you

If you are reading these words, I'd like to simply say – thank you.

Stepping through my first foray into writing, I've been surprised by my emergent love affair with the creative process. Talk about catching a girl off guard! Looking back, I'm doubtful that without this whirlwind romance, I would have found the courage to share my memories and reveal unspoken truths.

It has been powerfully energising and strangely cathartic.

Throughout our courtship, we've carved words from my thoughts and formed sentences from those words. The process has been instinctive, care free and rarely onerous.

Three years ago, I found myself stuck, in the lowest ebb of my life. Desperate to make sense of the turmoil I was in, I turned to non-fiction books. I devoured book after book at a frenetic pace, whetting my appetite for more. I found myself drawn to the words on each page, marvelled by the connection and inspired by their meaning. What struck me most, was the overwhelming sense of not being alone. Someone out there felt the same as me. It was a powerful revelation following an extended time of profound aloneness.

That is the gift I sincerely hope my story offers you.

Words that draw you to the pages, snippets of memories that stir your emotions and lessons that inspire you to find the courage to course correct your path in life.

All of us deserve to feel happy and fulfilled.

Including you.

Please enjoy.

Peta x

For Lewis

My Beautiful Mess

Peta Sitcheff

Panic
—

**"When I am silent.
I have thunder hidden inside"**

Rumi

Four days.

That was the time between when I shattered into a thousand pieces on the cold, concrete floor of an underground carpark and when I sat comforted by the warm embrace of Jo's red leather couch for the first time.

While I might have had chronic anxiety my entire life, on this particular Friday in June 2017, I was none the wiser. With the benefit of hindsight, I now know that it was clear from the crack of dawn that the day was never going to end well.

It's hard to explain how I knew it would be a bad day – I just did.

I woke up feeling what I can only describe as irritated and insular. As I blinked my eyes open, I realised my jaw was aching.

My Beautiful Mess

"I've been clenching all night," I thought. I wearily pulled myself into a sitting position on the side of my bed, desperately trying to ignore the niggling irritation that was starting to ping around inside my head. Like a buzzy fly trapped between a windowsill and a curtain, it was stuck and looking for a way out.

Dawn was breaking, and I caught a glimpse of the brightly coloured lights of the city skyline fading into the daylight hours. The whirring peak hour traffic had started to hum in the background and seemed to be growing louder and louder despite being almost a kilometre away. It felt like the traffic noise was closing in on me like a giant sound wave, filling my brain with painful vibrations.

I dragged myself upright and headed towards the bathroom, considering how as the sun rose it extinguished the lights from the buildings nearby. I wished to be far, far away from any city hustle and bustle. One day, but not today. Today I was heading into a crowded function room full of a thousand people cheering on AFL Women. No freedom of space there.

As I stepped into the bathroom I looked in the mirror and saw vertical red crease marks between my eyebrows.

    Time to start Botox my dear.

"I must have been frowning again in my sleep," I thought to myself, as I tried to smooth them out by pushing the skin on my forehead towards my scalp. The massaging touch of my fingertips on my face offered only a slight superficial relief to the tension in my skin. It was not enough to cushion the noise starting to pound inside my head.

On days like this, my brain was like a lotto barrel. It would start with one random ping pong ball, representing one anxious thought, bouncing around, desperately trying to find a way to free itself from the confines of the revolving barrel. As the minutes ticked by, another 'thought' ball would be added,

Peta Sitcheff

totally unrelated to the first. Then another, then another. Before long, what started as a lone random ball bouncing around on its own, evolved into the jumbled chaos of 47 balls. 47 random thoughts, chasing each other around the curved barrel walls, unable to escape, be tamed or comprehended.

I wish I'd known then that it's ok to risk exposing yourself to the elements of a cyclone of anxious thoughts. Hell, you can even coexist. As long as you learn how to weather the storm.

"I'll be right," I uttered to myself.

I stood in front of my wardrobe looking at the masses of designer clothes, stiff pleats exposing their newness, many with price tags still swinging off the sleeves. Attempting to throw a new outfit together stressed me no end. Clothes would sail from one side of the room to the other, until I would finally settle on an ensemble. I'd look at my reflection in the full-length mirror, happy with what was on the surface. On the inside, I felt awkward and wrong. I yearned to rip it all off.

So off the clothes would come. I would fling them into a crumpled pile of rejection on the bed in frustration. They'd be on, then off, then on again. The fabrics always felt a little too tight, a little too stiff – and just when I thought I could muster enough courage to lash out and wear something totally different, I'd relent. My shoulders would slump in defeat, my hands gravitating towards what was tried and tested – the familiar comfort of my loose-fitting threads. I hated tight clothes and had no idea why I bought them, they made me feel claustrophobic.

The irony was not lost on me that the act of buying these clothes filled my sails, and yet, dressing in them sucked the air back out and made me fall flat. Deep down I knew I was a fraud. I didn't deserve to be clothed in such beautiful & fashionable pieces. I wasn't responsible enough.

It was impossible to ignore lotto balls one to 15 now rattling around in

My Beautiful Mess

my head. A drum reminiscent from 'The Little Drummer Boy' joined the ensemble and started a familiar pounding percussion practice above my right ear, making it throb. The pattern was always the same.

I slapped on my make-up trying to avoid making eye contact with my reflection in the mirror.

> You know you can't hide from me. I'm watching you.

I angrily jammed my feet into my scuffed Valentino studded flats. At least with these, I'd look the part. I looked manicured on the outside and I figured as long as I did, nobody could hear the echo of my anxious thoughts on the inside. I grabbed my car keys off the kitchen bench and flew down the hallway towards the door, avoiding the mirror to my left on the way out.

I loved the secure confines of my car. It was a safe haven of things I could control, a place where no-one could burst my bubble. I could start the engine and drive wherever I wanted to go. I could flick on the seat heating and enjoy the soothing warmth across my lower back, while the distinctive scent of "new car" leather permeated my nostrils. I could choose from a smorgasbord of tunes to suit my mood, and I had a legal excuse not to pick up the phone. My brain had one task to focus on - drive from A to B safely.

That wintery Friday, I cruised around the lake to the nearby hotel. If you asked me to recall the direction I took, I couldn't have told you. I was on autopilot, totally trapped in my own head. I followed the snail trail of glowing red tail lights into the carpark of the hotel until it was my turn to gain entry permission from the candy-striper boom gate. Relief flowed through my fingertips as I released them from the steering wheel to catch the ticket the machine abruptly spat out at me.

I knew I was scraping the bottom of the barrel in more ways than one that day.

Peta Sitcheff

Snaking down into the concrete bowels of the underground carpark, my heart rate quickened as I tried to keep my gaze on the road immediately in front of me. I had always found ceilings of underground carparks ominous, like they were threatening to spontaneously cave in.

Keeping my head down, I walked quickly to the elevator, pounding the button frantically. I was eager to get back to visible sunlight.

As the lift doors opened, a wall of noise hit me like a large wave dumping me unexpectedly in the surf. Crowds of people, talking, laughing, calling, coughing over each other. Layers of noise and a mass of hundreds of people packed the foyer, shoulder to shoulder. My eyes were assaulted by bright lips splashed across faces and heels of dizzying heights. I glanced down at my flats in shame.

> At least I don't stand out in these.

A few bold blokes stood head and shoulders above the rest of the crowd but mostly, I was confronted by a sea of women.

Some were huddled in groups, others were standing on their own at the edge of the crowd, pretending to be busy on their mobile phone. As I tried to manoeuvre my way across the room, I was knocked in all directions by shoulder-padded strangers; oblivious to the physical blows their overenthusiastic gestures were imposing on those around them.

I turned sideways squeezing through narrow gaps in the crowd, stopping suddenly to accommodate a sudden arm thrust in front of me as a random introduction was made between two strangers.

> Breathe Peta.

I took a deep breath in for the count of four.

My Beautiful Mess

Thank god I am tall.

I allowed myself to imagine for a second what it would be like if I were a foot smaller in the land of giants.

No thanks!

With altitude came oxygen, something I sensed I would need in my reserves as lotto thought balls 16 to 30 were added to my spinning barrel brain.

Spotting my tall girlfriend's blonde head poking above the crowd, I made a beeline for the corner of the room where the relief of two walls beckoned. A tiny corner of solace amongst a suffocating mass of bodies and an untrained chorus of voices. Beads of sweat were forming on my upper lip.

Did I remember to put deodorant on? Christ, I stink.

"Uggh, breathe Peta, come on!" I murmured to myself as I exhaled every last breath out of my lungs.

The grand, gold doors to the ballroom heaved open revealing the army of white circular tables. What was meant to be euphoric, celebratory welcome music, sent me cowering into the corner.

"I'll meet you in there," I said to my friends. I made a dash to the restroom for a reprieve from the sensory overload pounding my brain. On challenging days, I became hypersensitive to messy noise. Cacophonies of loud or layered sounds that weren't meant to go together, were my enemy. The volume? Irrelevant. A phone notification, a screechy YouTube voice, on top of people talking, on top of a blaring TV or a loud radio, were like waving a red flag at a bull. Close talking, over crowd murmuring, over booming music... if you added in a mobile phone ring or a voice over a loudspeaker? Hell.

I'd find myself demanding quiet on the outside, to try to silence the screaming

Peta Sitcheff

voice on the inside of my head.

> What do you want? I don't know what I want. All I know is I don't need this. I can't do this.
>
> But I can't let anyone down. I've committed to being here.
>
> What's wrong with you? Look around you, everyone is enjoying themselves. Why can't you? That's right. You're just difficult.

I found the safety of my seat and breathed a sigh of relief. My own square foot of personal space for the next few hours in a room of 1000 people.

As the formalities began, we were welcomed by our host, a familiar voice from the weeknight news. The host's call for quiet initially fell on deaf ears, as free flowing wine turned up the volume dial on the audience. Our table was no exception.

I felt like the world was whirling around me, the layers of noise compressing my head like a vice. I made a feeble attempt to make idle chit-chat with my new dietician neighbour. She was most pleasant. I even found myself enjoying the conversation, providing light relief until we were rudely interrupted by a grating voice at the table. A lack of manners by our boozy friend jolted our free-flowing conversation into a different direction, both of us stunned by the lack of self-awareness and annoyed by the distraction.

"Do you think this top will go with my red skirt for Saturday night's dinner?" she demanded, thrusting her phone in front of my nose.

For me, it was the straw that broke the camel's back. It was one noise layer too much.

Balls 31 to 40 poured into my brain there and then and the barrel was given one heaving spin. I apologised profusely to the host mumbling something

My Beautiful Mess

about a migraine and stumbled for the exit. I had to get out and away from the wall of noise that was closing in on me before it trapped me in my own barrel.

Longing for the safe, isolated cabin of my car, I hot footed it out of the noisy room to the lift. Lunging for the button, I pounded it with my fist, willing the doors to open and swallow me into their silent boxed space. I knew I had one last hurdle to jump over.

While the descending ride to the car park offered a momentary escape, the tension within me mounted.

Stepping out of the lift, I fossicked desperately for the parking ticket in the bottom of my handbag. My fingers scraped the bottom of the bag, searching for its hard cardboard edges amongst the tissues, chewing gum and half decomposed receipts. Why I never put it somewhere I could access easily was beyond me.

Finally, I secured it. I pulled it out of the mess and held it up for the machine to swallow, taking a deep breath.

>Please let it be under $20.

I knew full well I was totally and utterly flat broke.

>$24. Fuck.

I slipped my card in anyway.

>I'll try in any case.

Declined. The card spat out. I slipped the card in again. Declined. The card spat back again.

Peta Sitcheff

I breathed deeply through my nose, struggling to take in enough oxygen.

> I can't go back into that room. How embarrassing. I need to get out. How can I get out? I'll just see what I can scrounge up from my bank accounts.

I picked up my phone. No wi-fi.

> Fuck.

By now I was struggling to breathe, tears tipping over my eyelids and forming not streams, but waterfalls down my cheeks. I slammed my hand onto the lift button and willed it to hurry and open. Up I went, to the ground floor where I desperately hoped to find phone reception. The doors slid open.

> Thank god.

I frantically logged into my accounts on my phone as my heart sank further. Every account had a balance under $10.

> Please can I scrape together enough to pay for parking?

I stood in the hotel foyer, wearing glittering Valentino studded flats and transferring $1 amounts from one account to another. I could barely pull together $24 to get my car out of the carpark.

> What an absolute farce you are Peta. A joke.

I managed to scrape together $32 by transferring into one bank account through my phone. It was all I had to my name. Now I needed an ATM.

"You'll have to go to the 7-11 over the road," the concierge said as he surveyed my hysterical state.
"OK, thank you very much," I said.

My Beautiful Mess

I quickly crossed the road to the 7-11, slipped my card into the ATM ducking my shoulders and keeping my head bowed the entire time. I was so ashamed.

I grabbed the cash and sprinted back towards the hotel. As I was running my left foot slipped out of its shoe and I flew forward landing on the pavement hard. My right hand flew out to break the fall. I jumped to my feet, ripping both shoes off and with Valentino's in hand, scrambled into the hotel. By now the tears were flowing, an unstoppable stream.

> Fuck the lift. Get me out of here.

I opened the fire escape and ran down the concrete stairwell of the carpark, the urine stench causing me to gag. I jammed my money into the ticket machine and jumped into the car, slamming the door with such force I'm surprised the rear view mirror didn't drop off. "Please close this chapter," I begged aloud to no one.

> Make this be over. I don't know what I'm doing.

I closed my eyes and rested my head on the steering wheel, desperately trying to catch my breath.

> What do I do? Where do I go?

My shoulders shuddered as my body was overcome by a convulsive outpouring of emotion. In between the sobs I gasped sharply, trying to take in oxygen, to catch my breath. In that moment it felt like 41 years of pent up emotion was exiting every crevice of my body. I cried with the shame of my financial neglect. I cried for the life I knew so well. I cried for my work family of 13 years. I cried for the insecurity of my unknown future. I cried with sadness for a failed marriage. I cried with guilt for my half-hearted parenting and with the fear of knowing – I no longer had any idea who I was.

The tears poured.

Peta Sitcheff

Recommended Reading
-

This Book will Change your Mind About Mental Health
Nathan Filer
Published by Faber & Faber Ltd (2020)

First, We Make the Beast Beautiful
"A new story about anxiety"
Sarah Wilson
Published by Pan MacMillan Australia Pty Ltd (2017)

My Beautiful Mess

Peta Sitcheff

Her
-

"Trouble is a tunnel through which we pass and not a brick wall on which we must break our head."
Tina Bruce

Those first moments after a summer sunrise were always blissful. Dawn tranquillity disturbed only by the laughter of a local male kookaburra, perched on his highwire like a king upon his throne. His piercing trills echoed through the valley of his kingdom and grated against my groggy head - all courtesy of the previous night's free flowing champagne.

How on earth am I going to do this for another year?

I laid staring at the ceiling fan, mesmerised by its slow revolution and calmed by its purring hum. I smiled as an image popped into my head of me belting out a verse of "My Way", into a makeshift, pepper grinder microphone the night before.

My Beautiful Mess

I'd always found New Year's Eve to be a night with more mixed emotions than spirits in the cocktails I drank. It was my bow-tying ceremony for the previous 365 days. One I either desperately want to cling to as though my life depended on it, or one I preferred to give a size ten boot up the backside, hurtling it like a comet into the stratosphere, never to be seen again.

Whatever my New Year's mood, I never seemed to shake the undercurrent of commercial reality that lurked back stage.

The evening before, as I'd jubilantly counted down the seconds until the pyrotechnic rainbows lit up the sky and the clock ticked over to 12:01am, the previous year's sales targets reset to zero. All the blood, sweat and tears, the millions of dollars - archived to the year prior.

As reality of a new selling year sank into my dehydrated brain cells, I pictured The Director standing over me, like an athletic coach ready to reset the stopwatch for one of their high-performance athletes.

"Ready, steady...SELL!" he'd bellow.

    Oh bugger off.

My jaw clenched as I pictured his suit clad image and heard the voice in my head.

This is exactly when it was likely to strike. I was on my annual family summer holiday for god sake and I still couldn't get away from either of them.

In a huff, I rolled my body over, taking in the deep blue undulating swell of Laguna Bay beckoning through the glass window. The sight was always medicinal, and a sense of calm instantly flushed through my body and mind.

Mum and I always said that our January 1st ocean swim washed away the previous year.

Peta Sitcheff

This year more than most, I couldn't wait to feel the ocean, warm with summer, against my dry Melbourne skin. Like a pod of frolicking dolphins, my family and I would dive through the waves amongst the schools of silvery bream, emerging out the other side collectively snorting salty goodness from our noses. It was like a massive dose of wellbeing in a single breath.

For 13 years, I'd endured and loved the high intensity training that came with my job as a sales professional. I was well acclimatised to deal with the terrain of the freshly vacated calendar year ahead. I'd developed the physical endurance required to sustain the 365 days (or 8760 hours) and built an armour of resilience that could deflect the personal blows. I had trained my fast twitch muscle fibres to react to a crisis in seconds while my emotions remained flatlined throughout. I knew how to keep my weaknesses hidden from competitive eyes and how to use my curiosity to build trust. My connections tight; knitted together with surgical grade, titanium strength.

I was a seasoned competitor and knew this playbook better than the topography on the back my own hand.

What I didn't understand, was the unfamiliar sensation that brewed within me. The starting gun had been fired, I knew it was a new year, but I felt odd. The buzz of excitement and swell of enthusiasm that usually had me chomping at the bit to race, just wasn't there. I didn't feel ready.

Instead, my bones felt heavy with dread. Not the best pre-race state for the 2016 ultramarathon before me. I felt like I was staring at an endless road, surrounded by hot, sandy desert, oasis shimmering on its surface. It was as though I was already dehydrated (which I was, courtesy of the champagne from the evening before). My enthusiasm buried under the tonne of work required to cross another finish line.

I had no idea how the heck I was going to find the energy to fire out of the starting blocks, let alone sustain the distance to December 31st.

My Beautiful Mess

But I had to. I had no choice. Too many people depended on me holding it all together. I had a routine to my day, a structure to my week and pattern to my year that I knew would deliver. The Director would be happy.

>I can't upset the apple cart.

I kicked off the crisp cotton sheets and reached for the Panadol on my bedside table. I could hear the sound of 10 year old feet padding up the hallway to my room, ready for Lewis's smiling face and twinkling eyes to peer around the corner of the door. He would be dragging me to the beach in minutes, innocently oblivious to my hangover.

I had a sudden sense of urgency to cool my boiling thoughts, the healing powers of the ocean magnetically calling to me.

Regardless of what mood the ocean was in at the time, it always delivered solace. A place of pure soundlessness where I could shrink into insignificance and feel connected to an indescribable something far greater than myself. Whether it was engulfed by the current of a lunar tide, full of the knots of a tangled seaweed mess or shimmering in crystal clear stillness, beneath the surface of the ocean, a salty therapy beckoned that could cleanse my soul and still my mind.

The ocean lent no oxygen to voices. It drowned out her voice.

I am not sure when "it" turned into a "she". Nor do I recall the first time it turned up. I never offered an invitation.

Initially, the presentation was the same. A curt instruction demanding to be heard. Not cruel, but certainly not gentle.

>That's not perfect. Work harder.

Peta Sitcheff

With a ferocious determination, I would work harder. Persevering at my chosen task until I received what I was looking for - recognition. If those who were important to me were happy, I had succeeded.

With time, it became more demanding. One instruction became two.

> What will other people think? You know their opinion matters.

Studiously, I obeyed every command. Naively, believing it knew best.

Then somewhere along the line, the tone changed. It was as though it became less of a teacher and more of a school yard bully.

> Everyone is watching you. Judging you. Waiting for you to choke.

She often turned up unannounced. Full of sass and demanding my attention.

Inviting herself on my annual family beach holiday was just rude. But manners or my convenience were never her priority.

> Oh Peta, you are such a sucker. It's so easy to throw you a hook and reel you in.

I could feel her tease, but I didn't know how to resist.

> You take the bait every time. You are so much fun!

It became a game to her. A cruel game. I felt inadequate, like I was never enough. I was convinced other people's opinions were more important than my own, obsessing over assumptions that had no truth. Meanwhile, she would continue her taunting, then lounge back and enjoy the show, amused by my tears. I knew I couldn't run away. I couldn't drown her out. Like a superhero with no known kryptonite – she seemed indestructible.

My Beautiful Mess

Through trial and error, I'd learned if I designed my life to be controlled and familiar, I could quieten her voice and if I was really lucky, I could even hibernate her for a while. I always trod cautiously though, careful not to poke the bear.

From time to time I wondered how we could become friends. Then life would take over and I'd swat the thought away.

She was always there, knowing full well she had the upper hand.

Recommended Reading
-

How do we Know we are Doing it Right?
"Essays on modern life"
Pandora Sykes
Published by Penguin Random House UK
(2020) p. 158

Peta Sitcheff

Feeling
—

"I've learned that people will forget what you said, people will forget what you did, but people will never forget how you made them feel"

Maya Angelou

In October 2002, the awful tragedy of the Bali bombings affected many Australians. I remember the stories in the news, the eye balls on the faces of the dead that would never blink again, in the newspaper.

Despite the haunting images, what I remember most about that time, was the smell.

Fortunately, I wasn't in Bali. I was oceans away in metropolitan Melbourne kick starting what would be a long and rewarding career of life lessons in the medical device industry. I had secured a new job with a company that sold high end vacuum wound care products and specialised burns beds. Two

My Beautiful Mess

months into that job, the tragic events in Bali unfolded, filling our airwaves and wallpapering our world. It was everywhere. The words in the newspaper, the voices on the radio, the drawn emotions on strangers faces in the street and in my case, it was at work.

I wasn't a nurse, nor did I have any clinical background. I had spent the past 2 years whisking in and out of GP clinics on the Mornington Peninsula dropping off antidepressant samples and dishing out free Viagra merchandise. I was rarely the sales representative who was turned away, conversely, I was at times even summoned for my brown paper bags full of little pale blue pills always requested 'for a friend'.

Suddenly, with very little formal training, I found myself among the trauma chaos of the bombings. My office that week was The Alfred Intensive Care Unit (ICU), surrounded by the most critically injured Australians who had been airlifted back. Charred skin, bandage covered faces stained by weeping wounds and empty spaces on white bed sheets recently vacated by blown off limbs. Wherever I looked my heart would jerk into my throat.

> How am I going to do this?

The reality of the situation I found myself in, sank in fast. While the patients were in transit from Darwin, we were alerted to race the burns beds into a dedicated ICU. Almost instantly, my brain kicked into gear to get on with it and get the job done. We had just two specialised beds available, for six patients. This bloody mattered and I had to get it right.

I arrived at the hospital to a media frenzy. Female journalists with perfectly manicured hair and made up faces were such a stark contrast to what I imagined was going on just one floor above them.

Dodging the sweaty camera men and jumping spirals of black cables, I walked briskly across the ground floor tiles making a beeline for the stairwell. My older colleague's voice rang in my ears from just a short time before:

Peta Sitcheff

Just look like you know where you are going, even if you don't. That way no one will stop you.

As I emerged from the stairwell out onto the floor of the ICU, I was hit by an eerie wall of tranquil silence. The air felt thick with the seriousness of the situation.

Step by step up the hallway, I could hear the faint sobs and whispers from the tiny family conference rooms. Tiny spaces crammed with wild emotion as mothers, brothers, sisters, fathers and lovers learnt of the patient's fate.

Buzzing into the ICU, I took a deep breath as the glass doors separated to be met with an orchestra of clinical sounds. The whooshing air of a ventilator, the pitchy ding of an empty intravenous drug infuser, the steady beat of the heart rate monitor. It was sensory overload.

Then there was the smell. I've been overwhelmed by hospital smells before. I remember being on the ward once when a nurse was changing her patient's infected heel ulcer dressing. The stench of pseudomonas had filtered through my nostrils and the blood had drained from my head at the same rate as the world closed in around me. Within seconds, I had hit the deck - out cold (much to the amusement of the beautiful elderly woman, lying there in her pearls with her rotting heel propped on a pillow!).

This time, I was armed. My blue surgical scrub pockets were loaded with white Kool Mints to suck on and distract my nostrils with peppermint fumes.

The smell of the ICU was hard to explain, particularly being a burns unit where the temperature was set above 28 degrees to assist with the unique thermoregulatory challenges confronting these patients. It was not sterile like an operating room. It had a festering sense of sickness about it - unwashed skin, musty sweat, urine, infection, oozy wounds and the odour of necrotising skin. It was unlike anything I had ever experienced and on my return home after a full day's work, no matter how much I scrubbed myself, I knew this smell would linger in my nostrils for hours afterwards. The mints didn't help.

For five days this was my office. I ensured the equipment was properly programmed, gortex sheets were in plentiful supply, supervised painful dressing changes and lastly, managed the occupancy of the burns bed. That was the hardest. As the days went by, many patients conditions deteriorated. On a Thursday they had a leg, by Saturday the leg was amputated. The kinetic therapy bed was reserved for the sickest of patients. Rented at $350 per day, it was the Rolls Royce of hospital beds. The latest electrical model with all of the bells and whistles. It could be programmed to automatically tilt its occupants, altering their body position to relieve the pressure on their skin. It would wake up lungs with its percussion therapy setting and stimulate wound healing via the whirring current of air whooshing through its air mattress. Its occupants were on high rotation. One day a patient was gravely ill, the next, they were dead.

We swapped the bodies on the bed with the death cycle.

As someone with no nursing experience, I had never been confronted by death like this before. There was nothing romantic or spiritual about a burns patient dying in an ICU department. It was hideous and stenching and as bad as I ever could have imagined.

All that stood between me and a patient in their final minutes was a flimsy cotton curtain. I slipped past one to hear a family sobbing by a bedside, while the head of intensive care barked orders at me to have that burns bed ready to move to Bay 8 at our earliest. I felt like a rabbit in head lights, nodding my head furiously, trying not to cry or to get into trouble for doing, saying or thinking the wrong thing.

Despite the shock, the combination of wild emotion, clinical urgency and deep sense of importance that came from being a member of this team, introduced me to a feeling of hyper-alertness I hadn't felt before. I may not have loved the smell but I loved being amongst the fragility of life and felt strangely alive in its presence.

That was Bali, then there was Sara.

That one patient I could never forget. Back at The Alfred, not long after the Bali patients had occupied the ICU space, I was called in to see a new patient. Her name was Sara. She was a young woman, similar in age to me. She'd experienced a terrible accident when a faulty gas heater exploded in her house. The scene was described in the media like a bomb site, literally. She had suffered third degree burns to 70% of her body and ended up in hospital for six months - the beginning of a lifetime of painful rehabilitation. Sara had burns covering both of her hands and required multiple finger amputations.

Our company had a specialised glove dressing that "accommodated" the amputation and was applied to both hands following surgical debridement. As the months passed, these dressings were able to be changed on the ward rather than the operating room.

Sara became a standing fixture in my day. I would pop by every 48 hours to make sure the electrical suction unit was functioning as it should, gently sucking the air from the foam, drawing rich oxygenated blood to her healing wounds. Over time, I was asked to supervise her dressing change, a procedure she had to be sedated for as the pain was intolerable.

Vacuum Assisted Closure (VAC) wound dressings consisted of a piece of thick foam placed over the wound. The foam was then covered with an adhesive plastic with a port. Over the port, you placed a tube that was connected to the suction device. When it was switched on, it sucked the air out of the foam and any wound fluid up the tube, into the canister. When it was on, the wound looked a bit like a vacuum-packed piece of meat from the butcher, but all you could see was the black foam. The negative pressure drew oxygenated blood to the area, minimising the risk of infection and promoting the production of new granular tissue – skin. For the hand dressing, it looked a bit like you were

My Beautiful Mess

wearing a black boxing glove.

One of the challenges with these dressings was if left for too long, the patient's granular tissue grew into the foam and would then get ripped off during the wound change. I can only imagine how incredible the pain was. Hence the sedation for Sara.

In spite of the uncomfortable clinical scene, one day there emerged an unexpected display of human connection that was so emotionally powerful, the memory is as vivid today as it was decades ago.

Sara was sedated but conscious and while the nurses attended to her physical wounds, I focused on the only way I felt I could help, by supporting her emotional wounds. I fixed my gaze on Sara's brown eyes as they welled with large glistening tears. One by one they fell down her cheeks onto her bandages, I sat by her side and never took my eyes away from hers. In the absence of touching and hand holding, I was doing everything I could to comfort her through my gaze. To connect with her and let her know I was trying to see the world through her eyes, to understand this was beyond painful and that she needed support. She needed to know she was not alone.

Nothing I could have said in that moment would have been remembered, none of it would have mattered because it wasn't needed. Before me, was a beautiful woman who needed to feel understood and not alone.

It was at that moment I learnt the importance of how we make people feel and the fact that in the hardest moments, it's never forgotten – which is what Sara would remind me of weeks later, when I went to visit her on the burns ward, following her release from ICU.

From that day, I vowed to never avoid someone's eyes because it made me uncomfortable. That would have said more about me than it would them. In and out of hospitals, every person in a wheelchair, every patient being wheeled into an operating room on a mobile gurney, I looked them in the eye and smiled. I did my very best to support them through my gaze and make them feel like more of a human than the UR number on their wrist.

That was my lesson. People never forget the way I make them feel.

It will be the most valuable gift I can ever offer.

Today's Reflection
-

Human connection fascinates me. The magical aura surrounding a spiritual connection between two souls whose behaviours mirror each other. So perfect is their synchrony.

I love the satisfaction that comes from unpacking how we are drawn to some and repelled by others. The rationale behind why we generously offer our trust to those we haven't known for long, unthreatened by their presence, yet to others, we guard it with our life, not giving an inch. Even if we have known them a lifetime.

In her exquisitely written book *Someone I Used to Know*, British woman Wendy Mitchell, describes the importance of how we make people feel, specific to her vulnerable community - people diagnosed with early onset dementia. As she discloses her diagnosis to her colleagues at the National Health Service for the first time, Wendy describes dementia to others as two bookcases. All of us, dementia or not, have two bookcases.

My Beautiful Mess

The first bookcase is the annals of our factual life. The top shelves are our most recent memories of - what we do, who we are and what our life is made up of. As the shelves get lower, we go back further in history until we reach the lowest bookshelf housing our earliest childhood memories. Dementia causes that book shelf to sway side to side – imagine an earthquake. The top shelves tumble first, the lowest shelf containing our oldest memories, remains.

The second bookshelf is our emotional life. It represents the way people who cross our path make us feel. The first impression they make and the lasting feeling that lingers in their fresh absence. For people with dementia, this bookcase remains rock solid.

Emotional connection is the oxygen to our soul. While discreet to the eye, its capability is powerful and can shake our bones. It's like a giant hug that screams "I hear you, I understand you, I've got you."

Emotional connections reassure that an arm will be offered if we stumble and that someone will give a damn if suddenly we are no longer there.

Recommended Reading
-

Someone I Used to Know
Wendy Mitchell
Published by Bloomsbury Publishing (2019) p. 97

Together
"Loneliness, Health & What Happens When We Find Connection"
Vivek H. Murthy
Published by Welcome Connection (2020)
p. 218-219

My Beautiful Mess

Peta Sitcheff

T-Junctions

"Be careful what you wish for, you just might get it"

Anon

"Private Number" flashed up on my mobile phone meant one of two things. Either there was a surgeon on the other end, fiercely protecting their privacy, or a hospital needed help with a VAC dressing urgently.

In this instance, it was the latter.

"Can you explain the patient's injury?" I asked the nurse from ward 2D at The Alfred Hospital.

"It's a motorbike accident," she replied.

Instantly, I could picture in my mind the problem she was trying to trouble shoot on the VAC unit. I had seen enough to vow to never get my motorbike licence.

Sure enough, the patient was male. The three long bones in his leg had collapsed under the weight of the motorbike he had lost control of on the motorway. The friction generated from his high speed slide had ripped the flesh from his leg as he was dragged to a standstill. Gravel, stones and dirt had embedded themselves into the wound, with his skin left behind on the

My Beautiful Mess

bitumen.

I hung up and made my way into the hospital. When I arrived, black VAC dressing foam engulfed the patient's leg. There were three long dressings in total. Two on either side of his upper leg, one on the lower leg. Each protected the fasciotomies from infection, as they worked to relieve the pressure of the swelling within the muscular sac. I could hear the air leak from the sealed dressing, hissing from the usual place. Nothing a bit of sticky OPSITE dressing couldn't fix. I applied it and instantly, the hissing stopped. The patient grimaced as the suction strengthened over his exposed nerve endings.

Generally, I would have stayed and chatted with the patient. They were always grateful for a fresh face in their day. Today I had to pardon my brevity and hop to it. I had to go. My brain skipping ahead and preparing for the job interview I knew I would now be late for.

My job was no longer challenging me, my brain becoming stale and this was one of those opportunities where I thought; "I have no idea about this, but I'll go for the experience. Nothing to lose."

Jumping in the car, I flung my handbag onto the passenger seat, littering the floor with lipstick and tampons in the process. "Damn" I thought to myself, cursing the unsettling mess.

With an 18 minute window to make the road crossing through metropolitan Melbourne, my optimistic hopes of a dream traffic run were rapidly fading. It was 2.42pm and the school zones had suddenly found their pulse, dammit.

With the determination of a rally car driver, I expertly manoeuvred my beastly Holden Commodore laden with sterile wound dressings through the suburban bends. I could hear cardboard boxes sliding from one end of the rear car seat to the other, thudding against the car door with the

Peta Sitcheff

momentum of each turn.

I dove down every backstreet I knew, strategically avoiding red lights and school streets filled with impatient parents in Toorak tractors. At 3pm every day they would stealthily comb the streets like ravenous great white sharks stalking their prey. Then "it" would appear, the perfect carpark space. One that would save the extra 50 metre walk in their glamorous lycra, to collect their darlings at the gate. I wish I had an undercover siren to whack on the roof and a megaphone handy to help clear my path.

'Make way!' I'd scream. 'Make way! Get out of my waaay!'

When I finally arrived, I looked at myself in the rearview mirror.

Christ.

Despite record travel time across town, I was still 12 minutes late, with no time to hunt for the lippy that had rolled itself somewhere under the passenger seat during the ride.

I'm more of a Chapstick girl anyway.

I dabbed my lips with a half-melted stick of Vaseline from the centre console. Desperately, I tried to rub out the bright red line across my forehead from the elasticised theatre cap I had been wearing only 30 minutes earlier.

"Here goes," I whispered aloud and took a deep breath as I snuck one last quick look in the mirror and jumped out of the car. My brain had totally vacated itself of the notes I'd carefully prepared the night before. I was going to have to wing it.

The Director greeted me warmly with a slight smirk on his face as he surveyed the blonde whirlwind before him. I was a stark contrast to his

My Beautiful Mess

orderly, neat and well controlled demeanour.

"How has your day been?" he asked.

A torrent of words spilled from my mouth faster than my brain could think. Before I knew it, my arms had joined in, flailing around like a crazy Italian mama trying to prove a point to her quietly spoken husband.

I had no doubt he received way more information and colourful adjectives than he cared for, as I dissected piece by piece, the traumatic wound debridement and dressing change I had just supervised at The Alfred.

As I left the interview I looked down and realised the buttons on my shirt were out of sync.

> Christ, I looked like a train wreck!

I could barely remember a word I had said, except one key moment. During the interview, we were interrupted by an orthopaedic surgeon's name flashing in capitals on The Director's mobile phone. I watched him carefully as he picked up the phone swiftly.

> Remember, always take a surgeon's call. They are that important.

I made a mental note, filing this information away in my cranial vault.

He spoke swiftly and assuredly, then hung up the phone.

"I can't imagine a surgeon would ever ring me on my mobile. What could I possibly have to say that they would want to hear? Don't they know everything?" I asked.

"Be careful what you wish for," he replied with a wry smile.

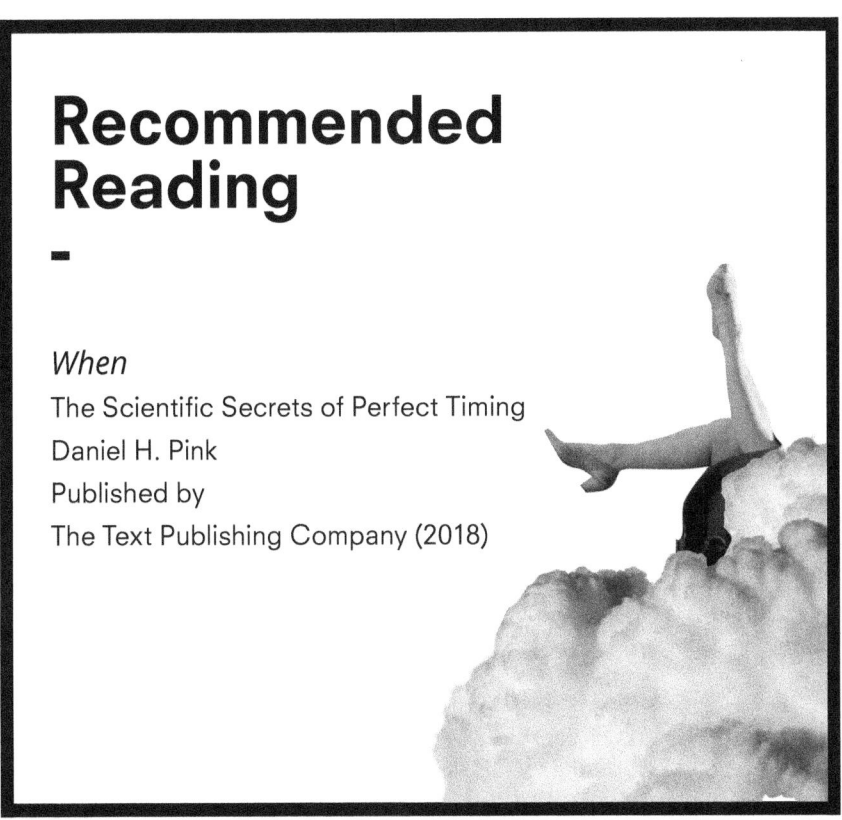

Recommended Reading
-

When
The Scientific Secrets of Perfect Timing
Daniel H. Pink
Published by
The Text Publishing Company (2018)

My Beautiful Mess

64 614
—

"Excellence is an art won by training and habituation. We do not act rightly because we have virtue or excellence, but we rather have those because we have acted rightly. We are what we repeatedly do. Excellence is then not an act but a habit."

Aristotle

I did or said something right in that interview as 24 hours later I got a call and was offered the job. Without fully understanding what was ahead of me, I accepted the position with a global medical device behemoth and enthusiastically threw myself into my new role with everything I had to offer.

It was a whirlwind.

My Beautiful Mess

There were days I felt like a marionette. Every part of me controlled by my puppeteer, the masked spinal surgeon. My emotions coiled and recoiled with their fluctuating moods. My pace quickened to match the urgency of their patient's plight.

For 13 years, I rode an emotional rollercoaster whose speed was turbo charged by a surgeon's call on my mobile phone. Their patients knew no boundaries, striking any time, day or night. A lumbar fusion, a cervical fusion, a deformity surgery, a trauma stabilisation or a reconstruction from an urgent tumour induced collapse of a vertebral body. I worked when they worked, which was 24 hours a day, 7 days a week, 365 days a year.

Against all of the typical wellbeing advice, I slept with my phone's blue glow glued beside my bed. The sound on. Always on. I didn't want to miss a call or let anyone down. A surgery booking meant business, business nudged me closer to my sales target and hitting that target meant – one big fat hefty bonus in the bank. Kerr-ching!

When the phone rang in the dead of a still night, my body reacted like it had been shocked with a defibrillator. I sat up startled trying to catch my breath, my heart pounding in my chest, quickly recovering to answer politely. "Don't be silly, it's no problem at all," I responded to the apologetic tones of the surgeon on the other end. And it wasn't. They were doing their job and I was doing mine. That was the path I chose.

If only spinal surgery patients presented during office hours.

I sold 64, 614 spinal implants over those 13 years. In terms of hours, I spent more than a full year of my life in the manufactured habitat of the operating room. A place of sterile hibernation from the day to day realities we saw on the nightly news.

The operating room was a world unto its own. A venue restricted for high

Peta Sitcheff

performance events carried out by a high performance team – there was no room for error. The stakes were high and success defined by the clinical outcome achieved.

It was an orderly world, painted black and white. Grey wasn't welcome, nor was it allowed. Each blue pyjama clad member of the surgical team was required to stay in their lane as they carried out their specific role. The patient's ID wristband was checked countless times throughout the procedure to confirm the correct human was in the room.

Nurses voices could be heard in the background as the patient was wheeled in. Together, the surgical nursing team would count out loud, noting every shiny steel instrument meticulously positioned on their trolley. They did this before each operation and again at the end, to make sure no foreign surprises were left behind.

The patient's operative site was cleanly shaven by the surgeon's assistant. The thick lines of a black sharpie tattooed the surgery location on their skin like an "x" on a treasure map. The masked surgeon then painted the operative site with a prep solution, usually bright pink or a rusty yellow – totally dependent on the artist's preferred colour. The surgeon, like an artist preparing the underpainting on their easel mounted canvas.

While the smell of alcohol filled the room and the underpainting dried, the surgical maestros donned their costumes. The room was filled with a selection of head lights, magnifying loupes, lead aprons and back braces for them to choose from. Then after a final pinch of the nose to seal their mask, they would head to the sink to begin their scrubbing ritual and prepare their hands for the performance.

Once head to toe in their pale blue protection, the masked spinal surgeon and their assistant veiled their patient in sterile drapes of the same colour palette. To an outsider, all that was exposed of the patient was the operative site, their personality paused, their lives hidden beneath a sea of sky blue.

My Beautiful Mess

Every clean, white gauze passed up to the surgeon during the surgery was counted one by one on the way in, and twice again in its blood-soaked form on the way out. No one left the room, most of all the patient, until the count was right. A missed piece of gauze in an obese abdomen the least favourite type of treasure to hunt.

Every mL of irrigation solution was measured and relayed to the anaesthetist. Every prosthesis packet eyeballed for size and cross checked to ensure what the surgeon asked for, was what was implanted into the patient. The process was strict and robotic. If something went wrong, someone or something was blamed. There had to be a reason and that reason would become a statistic.

Boxes were methodically ticked on operative charts as every step of the operation was legally recorded and hopefully, the desired clinical outcome achieved. Everyone played their role and there was a very clear line between what was right and wrong. If things didn't go according to plan the consequences were catastrophic.

Where did I fit in this sequence of events?

As the medical device representative, I too, was part of the pyjama clad blue army. First and foremost, as CPO (Chief Problem Solver) of my prosthesis and tool box. I wore many metaphorical hats aside from the surgical shower cap confining my blonde hair. At first glance, I appeared like a rover. Pacing the outskirts of the room, always within the surgeon's view. I wasn't scrubbed in or sterile, so I helped with the dirty jobs. I moved a pedal, fossicked for a CT scan, grabbed a sterile tray from outside of the room. I turned up the music, answered the phone and sometimes yes, mopped a masked surgeon's brow. It was never a good look when a pair of sweaty spectacles landed in an open lumbar spine wound.

I spoke only when spoken to, contributed to conversation when the mood allowed, but had to constantly read the room. I tried to never overstep my

Peta Sitcheff

mark. Knowing my place critical, always reminding myself I was the least important and most disposable person in that room. Regardless of how important I thought I was to a surgery, if there was a code blue, the one person who didn't have a role to play – was me.

Humility was never more important.

On paper, my success was measured by sales numbers. In my heart, I'd succeeded when my surgeon's heart rate barely rose above resting and they were smiling behind their mask as they closed the patient's wound. When the request came for the first deep tissue suture, you could feel the tension in the room lift, we were on the way out. We all knew what to do. The lights went on, the next patient called.

The most successful partnerships were defined by a deep sense of trust and respect.

I wasn't just selling my product and running out the door, I recognised the privilege that came with the invitation to be a part of the team in the operating room. The expectation was that I was the expert of my working product and while I didn't need intricate detailed knowledge for every surgery, when things went awry and a rescue situation presented, there was an enormous amount of gratitude in the room for that one "Get Out Of Jail" card I could provide.

I distinctly remember saying my "Hail Mary's" after a case with an inexperienced surgeon, grateful for paying attention in a weekend workshop when my mind was drifting towards the smell of coffee wafting in from the tables outside.

We were workshopping C1-2 posterior fusion surgery, a procedure where the patient was prone (on their stomach) and the aim to fuse two levels of the vertebrae together. Cervical spine refers to the neck and as humans, we have seven cervical vertebrae. This particular operation was right up the top of the spine, C1-C2 an area of increased surgical complexity due to the (very)

My Beautiful Mess

close proximity of vertebral arteries (a major blood supply to the brain) on either side. When you inserted a 3.5mm screw in a 4mm wide piece of bone, the margin for error was minimal.

When a surgeon booked a surgery the first domino was tipped, setting off a sequence of events between the booking and a patient on the operating table, full of titanium spinal hardware.

I'd like to say it was always a predictable linear journey, but of course it wasn't. Adding to the tension, the fact that once a booking was received, the countdown clock started ticking. I might have had three weeks, I might have had three hours, the rising stress levels were directly proportional to the plummeting minutes until the surgery went 'knife to skin' (started).

It was my responsibility to pre-plan with my surgeon what was required for the case and build the necessary equipment. This was then sent into the hospital and sterilised in time for the surgery. There could be three trays with 20 instruments or 20 trays with hundreds of instruments. Needless to say, at times it felt there were as many moving parts as the hot dinners I'd had in 45 years.

If the equipment was delivered the day before the surgery, I was treading a fine line. If it was the morning of, I was handling fire. If it was within hours, I was preparing myself to be no one's best friend and be on the record as the potential reason for a delay to surgery. Sterilisation took three hours minimum.

Once the starting bell rang, I became the "walking and talking" instruction manual.

Quite simply, you had to know your stuff.

At the time of this particular surgery, my knowledge was minimal, I hadn't seen many of these procedures. What I was accustomed to though, was

Peta Sitcheff

high pressured operating rooms. I figured if I learnt the facts well, I would be the best team member to service the case of this very new and young Neurosurgeon. It turned out to be the right decision.

The case progressed well, the masked surgeon relaxed and chatting freely. As it came time for instrumentation, I stepped up to the plate; ready to guide the surgical nurse through the workflow of instrumentation. We had four screws to insert, four holes to prepare, all under fluoroscopy or x-ray. The first two screws went in fine, the instrument sequence: power drill, tap, screw. The second two screws were a different story. On the extraction of the drill, the surgeon hit the vertebral artery. Rich, arterial blood filled the wound as the surgeon frantically tried to suction out the liquid and place pressure on the hole. In this circumstance, you couldn't see the ruptured artery, it was under bone. The only way to stop the bleeding was to put a screw in. The window of time we had where the surgeon would have visibility of the insertion hole was minimal. As soon as he took pressure off the site, it filled with blood. We had to work fast. Measure the length, assemble the screw and whack it in. As questions were fired quickly requesting screw diameters, thread types and lengths- I thanked Christ for my studious revision the evening before. As the dust settled, everyone breathed collective sigh of relief and the pulse rate of the patient steadied.

I looked up at the surgeon, sweat dripping down the side of his face, exhaustion in his eyes. We had one screw to go. He couldn't give up.

Off we went, repeating the same workflow, drill extraction, bingo. Again, came the blood, rich, red and pulsating. Now it was one thing to rupture one vertebral artery, but rupturing two was a different kettle of fish. Having already given the patient donor blood after the first rupture, the anaesthetist who was monitoring blood loss, started moving fast. There comes a point in any surgical crisis where the surgeon steps back and the anaesthetist's command takes over. Ultimately, they are the ones keeping the patient alive.

We went through the same steps. Screw inserted to stop the bleeding, we left

My Beautiful Mess

the rest of the construct for now (there were other less invasive implants to add to lock it down) and the vascular surgeon was called to repair.

As the patient stabilised, a unanimous sigh of relief fell across the room.

My role was complete and I stood back against the wall observing the high performance team before me. The previous tumultuous hour pushed to the back of their minds as they put their heads down to finish the job.

A day in an operating room was like running a marathon. Regardless of how slow the progress, or how complex the surgery, everyone kept moving forward. Hour after standing hour of intense concentration, wearing shirts soaked to the skin with sweat and shoulders laden with heavy lead aprons, could be relentless.

After surgery most of us would go outside, have a breather or maybe take the rest of the day off. For a masked spinal surgeon, that wasn't an option. They simply didn't have that luxury. It was a 45 minute turn around until their next surgery, the patient already being prepped in the anaesthetic bay.

Recommended Reading
-

Complications
"A Surgeon's notes to an Imperfect Science"
Atul Gawande
Published by Profile Books Ltd (2003)

The Talent Code
"Greatness isn't Born, it's Grown"
Daniel Coyle
Published by Arrow Books (2010)

Grit
"The Power of Passion and Perseverance"
Angela Duckworth
Published by Penguin Random House UK (2016)

FLY!
Life Lessons from the Cockpit of QF32
Richard De Crespigny
Published by Penguin Random House Australia (2018) p.94

My Beautiful Mess

Peta Sitcheff

No
-

"No one can make you feel inferior without your consent"

Eleanor Roosevelt

Sometimes I'd think it would be so much easier to be "scrubbed in" as a part of the sterile surgical team. I could assemble my own overengineered instruments, load the fiddly screws onto screwdrivers myself and have the instruments at the ready to keep up with the pace of the surgeon. I could have control.

Then I thought better of it, grateful for the shield the surgical nurse provided between my masked spinal surgeon and me.

I'd bottle the blood of these individuals. They were the linchpin of a successful spinal surgery and had the potential to make or break the case. It was their performance that reflected my own. How well I educated them was directly proportional to the level of trust in our connection. Like a young child within arm's reach of a shelf stocked with Waterford crystal, I wasn't allowed to touch. I delivered instruction always without touching.

My Beautiful Mess

Occasionally you'd get a poor soul who had been allocated a shift with a masked spinal surgeon they had never met, doing a procedure they had never seen, let alone understand. I dabbed more than a few teary eyes of surgical nurses. I remember one case where English was the surgical nurse's second language. She couldn't keep up with the speed of the impatient surgeon, her dainty double gloved hands trembling as she struggled to load the fiddly screws tightly on the screwdriver. Rather than work with her, the surgeon thought ramping up the pace and raising his voice would be a more effective strategy to bring out her best. It wasn't.

Tears streamed down her face as she tried desperately not to show her emotion. I could see in her eyes she was wishing the experience over. She was stuck there, with him, until the surgery finished. If I could read minds, I have no doubt her running thoughts would have told that surgeon where he could shove his screw, in her language of choice.

At least when I was not scrubbed I had a leave pass. I was not trapped to the confines of that room. Hours on end, standing on my feet, bladder bursting. My shoulders weighed down by the heavy lead apron that protected my vital organs from beaming radioactive rays.

I was still on a leash, just one with a bit more length than the sterile surgical team. I could escape for small bouts of relief from the tension that gradually mounted with the degree of surgical difficulty and I could distance myself from the explosive frustration that ricocheted off the walls when something went horribly wrong.

That didn't mean I could be complacent. Once the smell of burning flesh filled the air from the diathermy dissector, I had to be switched on, focused only on centrestage - the operative site. Everything that happened from then on, only mattered if it helped me deliver the best outcome possible for my surgical team and their patient.

I tried to be acutely aware of every cue I could interpret to make up for the

Peta Sitcheff

one sensory input I lacked - vision. Unless a surgeon was working under a microscope with a screen replicating their work, I couldn't see what they saw. I was reliant on what I could see on the surface and what I could hear, to help me understand the lay of the land.

Idle chit chat with the anaesthetist helped gauge the masked surgeon's mood. The instruments used indicated their place in the sequence of events. The tone of the surgeon's voice allowed me to sense their urgency. The movement of their eyes, their levels of concentration – every detail helped me understand.

Asking for the instruments that sat on the sidelines 'on hand' told me the surgery would take a little longer than anticipated and that a complication had occurred.

Every surgeon did the same operation differently. The procedure might have been the same, but that was where similarity ended. Setting them up for success depended on compliance by the entire team to their personal requirements. What they said goes. What they wanted, they got.

Every preference was noted in a surgeon's set-up folders and each time, the room set up accordingly. No excuses.

The masked surgeon in Operating Room 2 liked to stand on the right side of the patient, the one in Operating Room 3 stood on the left. One liked a pressure mat to stand on.

"Not the black mat, the blue mat... you know the one!" he'd order.

The other would need a stool. The room temperature had to be at 17°C for one, 20°C for another. Fluoro lights off. Fluoro lights on. Music on. Music off. Access via one door only. Loved a crowd. Chatter fine. Silence only.

These constants were their perfect conditions and enabled each surgeon

My Beautiful Mess

to manage their stress triggers. Like a professional tennis player with a disciplined pre-game routine, they too had their similar rituals that needed to be repeated for every operation, to psyche them into their best mindset for the task ahead. Call it superstitious - it wasn't up to anyone to judge. I knew one surgeon who had a rule of threes. If three things went wrong before a surgery, it would be cancelled. Even if the patient was in the anaesthetic bay waiting to be wheeled into the operating room. He wouldn't take the risk.

I had another surgeon who for instrumented cases, was very particular about the medical device representative he would allow in the room. A quiet achiever to those who didn't know him well, a raving comedian after a few lagers for those who did. I never appreciated my value to him until the day I resigned, and he described me as his Valium.

"When you turn up, I just know everything will be fine and if it isn't, you will find a way. I trust you," he said.

Each to their own.

The more a surgeon operated in a state of calm focus, the better they could manage the unexpected challenges and control their reactions. I would continually watch for stress cues. A grinding jaw, a reddened neck, an abrupt quiet, a change in tone, a barking voice to turn down the music. All signs that concentration was required and to let everyone in the team know to anticipate change. What came next varied person to person. Some kept their cool, internalised the pressure and worked through the scenario calmly, but others were less rational.

Like anyone on a bad day, any surgeon could let fly and have difficulty managing their emotions. Given the pressure they were under, it was easy to excuse. However, having seen many a masked surgeon under extreme stress, I am now of the firm belief that it is not an excuse to treat people poorly. For many, the intimidation it created silenced those around them. Witnesses feared the repercussions of speaking out with a different point of

Peta Sitcheff

view. Even if they were in the right and the surgeon was in the wrong. The power dynamic offered an interesting predicament.

I remember standing in an operating room once, watching a surgeon preparing a screw hole in a vertebral body, looking at the instrument on the X-Ray screen and thinking to myself, "This isn't the level we are doing."

I discreetly checked the patient consent. What was consented wasn't what I was looking at.

> Crap. What to do? Surely, he'll notice. Nope. He's going down the wrong path...

I took a deep breath, stood behind the surgeon, and then with a very small step closer, whispered quietly, "Doctor are we doing an L3-4 fusion today?"

Knowing I wouldn't speak up unless I was genuinely concerned, he looked at the screen. He quickly whipped the instrument out.

"Thank you. I've been operating since 2am," he said wearily.

> Phew.

No one was infallible. Finding your voice and having the confidence to use it respectfully could be the difference between a great outcome and a clinical disaster. In an operating room antiquated power dynamics might be assumed, but in reality, all humans were equal; the staff, the surgeon and the patient. It was OK to be wrong.

Fortunately, poor surgeon behaviour was reserved for the minority. However, if I was on the receiving end of an emotional pummelling, it made for a pretty crappy day.

I wasn't an employee of the hospital, nor was I under the protective roof of a corporate bullying policy. My role fell between the cracks and at times I was expected to tough it out if I wanted more of the masked surgeon's business. It could be brutal and often unfair.

I had one customer who I spent a lot of time with over the years. He was quite the perfectionist. Some may have described him as a narcissist but beneath it all he was one of the easiest to manage because he knew exactly what he wanted.

"I do it exactly the same way every time," he'd say in a moment of frustration shaking his diathermy in my direction.

He wasn't wrong. I used to play a game in my head and challenge myself to be a step ahead of him, the nurse always at the ready with the next instrument, our screws always pre-calculated and preloaded. On a good day, his workflow was never disrupted, his rapid pace never slowed. When everything went well we flew as one team.

On the other hand, when the shit hit the fan, it splattered the room and covered everyone in the process. Whether it was your problem or not, it was made your problem. Someone had to be blamed and the entire room would wear the burden. At the time, my equipment was pretty clunky and antiquated. There were many days I prepared to duck as I waited for him to hurl a clunky piece of stainless steel in my direction. Whether he wanted to believe it or not, the equipment worked pretty well in his hands.

On a day that wasn't going so well, frustrations boiled from a slow bubble to a volcanic eruption. Expletives spewed left, right and centre. Instead of being objective and reasonable, he made it personal, attacking me where it hurt knowing full well there wasn't a thing I could do about it there and then.

He needed to blame someone and that someone was me. There was a tone in his voice that would change and make my blood run cold. I knew what was coming and would brace myself for the verbal onslaught guaranteed to be fired in my direction.

It would start with a tirade of whining directed at me, shaming my organisation. Then the whining would crescendo into a bellow. The finale, was the gown being ripped off, stuffed in the closest bin with a punching fist and the theatrical (yet predictable) storming out of the operating room. The tension in the room would follow him on the way out like a southerly icy gust of wind.

As the door closed behind him, there would be silence. Only the hissing of the sucker could be heard. The rest of us would be left standing there, reading each other's minds.

>Here we go again.

We were grateful for the small window of reprieve that came with his momentary absence.

The patient would be lying there on the table, oblivious to the surgeon's antics. Their open wound exposed, the surgical assistant putting the hissing sucker to work, slurping up the blood as it pooled to prevent it from spilling onto the floor.

>Talk about throwing the toys out of the pram.

The first time this happened, I stood in silent shock.

>For the love of god. Who treats people like this?

"This...is a piece of shit!" he'd scream. The force of each word slammed me backwards until I hit the wall. Forgetting my own advice, I took every syllable personally. The tears stung my eyes.

The first chance I had, I fled to as much privacy as a communal changing

My Beautiful Mess

room toilet cubicle could offer. I sat on the toilet trying to muffle my sobbing, wishing desperately I didn't have to go back in there again for the next case. I don't know why I bothered.

The job could be totally thankless.

Fortunately, I didn't need to say much. That surgeon copped a dressing down from his anaesthetist and the Neurosurgical nurse unit manager. As upset as I was, I wasn't going to give him the satisfaction of not having to face me, so I fronted for the next case (thankfully a much simpler one), my make-up washed off from the tears. He offered a sappy over cooked apology. It was accepted but never forgotten.

Interestingly, a year later, a similar incident occurred but over the course of that year, my armour had thickened. I had very firm boundaries of what was and wasn't OK and had no qualms in articulating them. I am not sure why I was different. Perhaps I wasn't holding onto the business so tightly? My "No Dickhead Policy" had kicked in. This time when the verbal barrage started and he hurled insults towards the company – I wasn't going to accept it. The blame train for a problem that occurred because he was rushing through what he was doing, was no longer going to wash.

"Are you under control?" I asked my scrub nurse, who was so embarrassed on his behalf.

I knew given her experience she was. She nodded silently.

"With all due respect doctor, I'm not listening to this," I said. And with that, I turned on my heels and walked out leaving him to sort out the rest of the surgery.

It was unexpected for all and the best kind of "fuck you" I could give without saying the actual words.

Fortunately for the rest of the team, it did shut him up. His behaviour wasn't okay. He had pushed me too far and I was proud that he knew it.

Recommended Reading

The Fearless Organisation
"Creating Psychological Safety in the Workplace for Learning, Innovation and Growth"
Amy C Edmondson
Published by John Wiley & Sons Inc (2019)

Crucial Conversations
"Tools for talking when Stakes are High"
Patterson, Grenny, McMillan, Switzler
Published by The McGraw Hill Companies (2012)

Leadership the Eleanor Roosevelt Way
"Timeless Strategies from the First Lady of Courage"
Robin Gerber
Published by Portfolio (2003)
p.171

My Beautiful Mess

Humanism

—

"Emotionless facts won't engage with people who are emotional beings"

Peta Sitcheff

My job offered a smorgasbord of personality labyrinths to explore, none more so than the masked spinal surgeon, especially the neurosurgeon. Each were unique individuals who I respected deeply. Their commonality, sharing the need to cope with the complex challenges their specialty presented; realities the everyday person could never comprehend.

Neurosurgery is more than a profession, it is a commitment for life for both the surgeon and their inner sanctum. Their training is relentless and at times, unforgiving. After deciding on their specialty of choice, they race their peers for selection into a six year highly specialised training program. Around the age of 35, they emerge as a fully qualified consultant finally able to call their own shots. While their peers from secondary school have been climbing corporate ladders, nesting their growing families and enjoying the freedom of cashed up adulthood, the neurosurgeon is only just taking the reins of their professional destiny. They are finally; in control of their time,

My Beautiful Mess

have a say in the life sacrifices they are willing to make and let's not forget about the accumulated study debt they can begin to pay off.

But there is something else that comes with this newfound professional freedom. Responsibility for the risk that comes with just having an off-day. One caused by the weariness from a disturbed night sleep, woken by their sick child. Where the smallest slip of a scalpel can impair another for the rest of their life - or worse.

I distinctly remember one burly neurosurgeon looking totally defeated, almost childlike, as I arrived for a case with him one Monday morning. His previous craniotomy didn't go well. He had just come from a family meeting with a Mum and Dad to advise he couldn't remove as much tumour as they had hoped from their 19 year old daughter's brain, it was inoperable. For a few short minutes, he removed his surgeon mask and exposed the human who cared, who connected and who like all of us, had the capacity to hurt.

I learnt to be constantly mindful of what I was walking into. Reminding any new colleague, "You can't take it personally. We have no idea what conversation they have just had."

A masked spinal surgeon might be the CEO of their operating room, but beneath the qualifications and ego was an emotional human being who felt and suffered just like the rest of us. There was nowhere to hide under the bright lights of the operating room stage.

One very early morning, I received a phone call from a surgeon. Hearing the phone ringing as I was dripping fresh from the shower, I flew across the bedroom, wet footsteps imprinting the carpet in my wake. I was ready for a last-minute demand for an all day operating list, instead all I heard on the other end of the phone, was sobbing. This person wanted to meet me as soon as I could get to the hospital. They would speak with me then. An hour later, there we sat in the corner of the empty cafeteria, bitter hospital coffees in hand, plates clanging in the background as the patient breakfasts were

Peta Sitcheff

loaded onto the giant shelved trolleys, ready for the trip to the ward.

He sat with his back to the room as he poured his heart out. It was a gut-wrenching scenario, one that would turn his personal life on its head. This usually bold as brass performer, the lead actor of his operating room, was a meek shadow of his usual self. Frightened, confused and deeply hurt, he wiped the tears falling from his eyes as he re-counted the last few days of his life.

"You are the only person I have told" he said quietly. I listened intently, totally perplexed.

Why me? I don't understand why he's sharing this with me.

I looked down at his hands.

A full day of surgeries starting in 20 minutes and his hands won't stop shaking like a leaf. Not ideal for holding a scalpel. Not good.

Suddenly very aware of the pressure I was under, I questioned what he would do next. "Are you sure you are up to operating?" I asked, unable to hide my concern.

Surely, he will cancel his list?

My worry wasn't only for him, it was for the first patient on his operating list who would be anxiously waiting upstairs for their surgery to start.

"It will take my mind off it," he responded.

I don't believe you and I don't think you believe you either.

"OK, your third case is with me, so I will see you after lunch. You don't have to do this, you know?" I said gently, trying to offer reprieve.

My Beautiful Mess

"I'll see you soon" he said, as he turned and trudged his way to the operating suite upstairs.

    I tried.

All I could do was settle in and wait my turn on the operating list.

I arrived after lunch in plenty of time to prepare for my surgery.

    My part has to be perfect today.

We unwrapped the instrument trays and set up the heavy orthopaedic equipment for the surgery. The entire team was in full swing, including the patient, yet the surgeon was nowhere to be seen.

    Where is the person who's going to repair this spine and eliminate this poor patient's excruciating back pain over the next three hours?

As the person most redundant, I offered to go and find the surgeon.

With firm intent, I rapidly paced the halls searching every private room in the operating suite I knew. No cigar. His mobile rang out, again and again.

I had one last place up my sleeve. As I walked up the lonely corridor, lined with carpet stains, I caught a glimpse of the hidden surgeon up the shadowed end. Seeing me, his eyes pleaded with mine silently: *I can't.*

    I know.

I offered to take the afternoon's pressure away and discreetly help him to his car.

Peta Sitcheff

Peering through the small square glass window in the operating room door, I could see the patient, amongst the bustle, still awake and waiting for that reassuring pre-op conversation with their surgeon. I peered my head around the flimsy curtain of the anaesthetic bay, looking for the anaesthetist, who was anxiously looking at the clock, hoping for an early get away.

"Where is he?" the frustration mounting with each word. Without saying anything at all, I let my eyes do the talking. "Do we need to give the patient a lolly?" I was asked. I nodded. "Understood."

And like that, the perfectly laid, unused equipment set up in the operating room was dismantled and sent for decontamination. No questions asked.

The patient, back to the ward. Their spine saved from the shaky hand, for today.

That day my surgeon needed a safe place where they could be human. Where their rawest vulnerabilities could be exposed in a world where they were expected to have all of the solutions.

Like all of us, they didn't always have the answers to their own problems.

Today's Reflection

Sometimes I think I'm a glutton for punishment, but I just can't help myself. Like a moth to a flame, I am drawn to difficult personalities.

I love unpacking their copious layers. I've always thought that if someone appears difficult on the surface, the likelihood is you don't yet understand them well enough.

That is how I see complex personalities, as original ancient artefacts, fossils, desperate to be discovered and understood.

They are like a challenge that presents as a big, juicy onion. To understand them, you have to patiently peel back layer by layer, until you reveal the instruction manual on how they operate. The peeling process isn't easy, it can be eye watering. There will be tears of joy, tears of frustration and tears of anger as you ride the emotional rollercoaster that accompanies the challenge, but once you understand the onion, you come to realise that beneath it all, they are human at the core.

Peta Sitcheff

Recommended Reading
-

Being Mortal
"Illness, Medicine and What Matters in the End"
Atul Gawande
Published by Profile Books (2014)

Elegantly Simple Solutions to Complex People Problems
Jaemin Frazer
Published by Jaemin Frazer (2018)

Principled
"10 Leadership Practices for Building Trust"
Paul Browning
Published by University of Qld Press (2020)

My Beautiful Mess

Peta Sitcheff

Choice
—

> "We all make choices, but in the end our choices make us"
>
> Andrew Ryan

Generally, I liked to spend Wednesday nights on the couch with a glass of Chablis watching Gruen, not lying on a hospital gurney with the face of a masked spinal surgeon peering over me, catheter protruding from my long, skinny arm.

But that's where I found myself after an excruciating 24 hours spent lying and crying on the cold kitchen tiles unable to move. Acute disc ruptures hurt. A simple twist in the car to pick up the shopping bag and explosion! Burst disc guts wrapped where they weren't meant to be - around my L5 nerve root. The pain was searing.

But I wasn't crying just from the pain. I was resigning myself to the fact that the flight to the Gold Coast Lewis and I were meant to be on the next day, wouldn't be happening. I couldn't sit in a kitchen chair, let along sustain a two hour flight. We had been looking forward to our first Easter together with

My Beautiful Mess

Mum's extended family in I couldn't even tell you how long. We didn't know at the time, it would be Nan's last.

The irony. After 13 years spent in spinal surgeries, the day after the night on the kitchen floor, I was wheeled into the same operating room I usually worked in, with the same team of people I used to work with.

> Gosh it's so different from this view. Faces are kinder, softer. Woah! The lights are brighter. I don't have any job to do except lie here. No one is relying on me for anything. There is no pressure. I am surprisingly relaxed. Everyone is making a fuss over me. Hang on, that's the difference. Everyone is here for me. I'm the patient.

I took an enormous sigh of relief as I drifted off into my medical induced snooze, calm in the comfort of knowing I was in the right place and in the wonderful hands of someone I trusted.

Trust. I never appreciated its importance as a patient until my surgery. The only reason I knew who to trust was because I knew so many spinal surgeons. Many, now dear friends. In that moment on the operating table, I trusted that every decision my surgeon made on my behalf, was what was best for me. Not what was going to make the best x-ray for his colleagues to see at the upcoming department radiology meeting.

I think now of all of the surgeries I attended over the years and realise how small a piece of the puzzle my role was. If a patient's episode of care stretched over 90 days (conservatively), I was merely in the picture for a few hours. Officially, I wasn't allowed in the room until the patient was asleep. Most of the time, they didn't even know I was there. I had no idea what their voices sounded like or what their favourite colour was. I didn't know if they had family or how scared they might have been for what they were about to go through. The only detail I knew, was what I could read on their patient ID sticker.

Peta Sitcheff

Facts with no emotion.

I was one small part of what was often a very complex patient equation that the surgeon was responsible for solving. A part that didn't have the added complication of personality, medication, rehabilitation compliance or accompanying co-morbidities. I supported doing what it took to achieve the outcome the surgeon wanted, on a body that for those hours, was anonymous.

I was the only person in the room other than the patient, who didn't have a formal clinical qualification. Nor was I accredited or employed by the hospital. I had no legal responsibility in the operating room. However, I was incentivised to sell my product.

Without doubt, I've rode the lucrative waves of commercial success. However, always, my team and I took great pride in the integrity within which we conducted ourselves. Patient first. Always.

"Let's bring our A game," we'd say. We tackled complex cases together as a team. We worked incredibly hard to ensure our surgeons had a learning experience that set them up for success and gave the patient the best outcome possible. We left nothing to chance and managed expectations closely. A learning case was exactly that - a process of learning. There was some trial and error, missteps and unfortunately, occasional disasters.

Innovation of medical technology would ebb and flow with the oscillating depth of regulatory red tape. Generally, a young surgeon's baseline operative technique was based on what they learnt during their training. The more they performed a surgery a certain way, the greater the value of their experience bank. As their brain and hands became more familiar with a particular surgical technique, they developed neural pathways that improved their conscious competency. They used less of their reactive brain, more of their observing brain and were more likely to effectively troubleshoot based on their ability to recognise "patterns" from their previous experience.

My Beautiful Mess

It would become automatic.

Familiarity offered security. It reduced risk and set them up to deliver the best clinical outcome for the patient.

When a new surgical technology came to market, it could involve anything from a slight modification of current technique, to a more radical process that required learning an entirely new procedure.

Change, regardless of enormity, would introduce risk. A surgeon's willingness to change their surgical technique was directly proportionate to the amount of risk they were comfortable exposing themselves or their patient to.

A new surgical technique involving new technology is taught through the medical device industry. The process of learning slow and delicate, requiring patience and tolerance by all.

Initially, learning cases tended to be slow and clunky, as the team grappled with the workings of the foreign equipment. The scrub nurse had to learn how to assemble the instruments as well as keep up with the surgeon's pace, while the surgeon and their assistant had to understand the instrument function, all the while looking for the comfort that familiarity would bring.

I always felt like I was being pulled in every direction during those labour intensive hours. Helping the nurse find an instrument amongst a stack of heavy metal trays, answering a question asked by an impatient surgeon. My eyes were everywhere. A pair in the back of my head would have been handy on more than one occasion. Always, I had one on the surgeon, making sure they weren't forcing something that wasn't meant to be forced. Ready to leap to the rescue or intervene with a respectful, "Doctor, before you do that..." to prevent a disaster. I detested disasters under my watch.

Constantly, my brain made mental notes of changes required before their next surgery.

Peta Sitcheff

T-handles not straight handles. Straight not curved instrument. Leave the ratchet off. For Christ's sake don't give him that instrument again. I can't forget. It will look like I don't care.

It often wasn't until the first closing suture was called for, that I would feel my body relax for the first time in hours. In those cases, I became a people manager, a logistics supervisor, an educator, a coach, a counsellor, a mood stabiliser, a cheerleader, a solution provider and an endurance athlete all rolled into one. The masked spinal surgeon didn't just book my equipment, he booked me, along with my armamentarium of capabilities and bags of positive energy I brought into the room.

At times I felt like a tight rope walker, treading a fine line between where my responsibility started and where it ended. It was a privileged and often difficult position to be in. A surgeon placed their trust in me to carry them across the learning ravine and bridge the gap between what they knew and what they had yet to learn. How did I draw the line? It wasn't always easy. Particularly if stress levels were escalating and the room was emotionally charged. I had to be clear on what was and what wasn't OK. I had to have boundaries in place that I needed to respect and adhere to. If I didn't, no one else would either.

As a Medical Sales Device Representative I was considered a product expert, not the operation expert. It was OK to admit I didn't know something. My communication needed to be factual and objective because that was the information my surgeon was relying on to make their intraoperative decisions. Often, I faced or saw other representative's faced with gaps in their kits. Missing implants that hadn't been restocked from a previous case. It was a T Road junction. I had to either decide to let the surgeon know at the start of the case, manage his expectations and allow the boiling temperament to simmer or, run the gauntlet. If I decided against telling them, I had to hope like hell they didn't ask for that size implant. If I sprang the surprise on them intraoperatively in all likelihood the shit didn't just hit the fan, I could be given

My Beautiful Mess

a one way ticket out of the operating room at the end of the case.

It was up to me how closely I toed the line. Treating it like a charged electrical fence and staying well away, as often as I could, was my strategy of choice.

Intraoperative decision-making was the responsibility of the surgeon as legally as it was practically. They couldn't make the best decisions without all available information. I had a responsibility to tell them what I knew, regardless of how awkward the conversation. Once they knew, they could do what they wished. If they went off script, it was their choice. After all, I couldn't see what they could see.

What I could and did do, was cover my bases. I'd choose my words wisely, ask as many questions as I could to understand what the surgeon was trying to achieve and ensure the options offered were heard clearly by everyone in the room. Everyone.

A surgeon wanted to know I had their back but that equally, I knew my place. Above all, they needed to know that their priority - the patient - was my priority.

The competitive landscape within the industry, was a darker corner of the operating room. One where boundaries were pushed, and representatives felt the need to attend surgery not because the surgeon needed them there. Nor did the nurse. They were there to "protect their turf" from a competitor. They were in the room because if they weren't, they wouldn't be invited back. Their competitor would be instead, their business lost.

It's an unfortunate fact that a minority of surgeons wouldn't let you forget.

"If you want my business you need to turn up" they'd say. Never mind it was another body in the room contributing to infection risk. Some operating rooms could have up to five medical sales representatives at a time. All lined up against a wall as though they were in a viewing gallery. They looked like

Peta Sitcheff

an audience to the surgeon's operating theatre. Aptly named, given in the 18th Century operating theatres were exactly that - places of entertainment for public viewing. It was behaviour better reserved for the school yard. If only the patients knew.

I remember in the early days of the job standing patiently in an operating room one Monday afternoon. I was there for my implant to be used. Booked, confirmed and pre-planned with the surgeon. There was another type of implant being used in the surgery, provided by a different company. One of their senior representatives walked in the room. We didn't know each other well. As the surgery progressed, directly behind the surgeon, he started opening trays for a product in direct competition to mine and placing them on top of my trays.

> What is happening here? Have I missed something?

I had only confirmed with the surgeon he was using my implants half an hour earlier before he scrubbed. The scrub nurse took the trays, looked at me and shrugged her shoulders.

Another T-junction moment. I could turn right, stay quiet, keep my trap shut and potentially lose the business or, I could turn left, pipe up and confirm the surgeon's intent. Taking a deep breath, I chose left. The surgeon looked at me slightly annoyed.

"Yes, I told you that earlier," he said. Fortunately, the scrub nurse came to the rescue and had the surgeon turn around to see the hastily placed trays towering behind him.

"I'm using Peta's implants today," he spat into his mask.

Finally, I exhaled.

These mind games went on because they were allowed. Some surgeons enjoyed the power trip, playing one company off against another and keeping the representatives on their toes. It was a dynamic driven as much by the surgeon as it was the representatives. It was unhealthy, unhelpful and detracted from the priority in the room – the patient. Managing the competitive landscape and navigating the mind games could test the strongest of ethical beings. In the end, it became the business I would choose not to have.

"Choice" being a card that any sales professional has the luxury of being able to play.

I think back to a Saturday morning surgery booking. It was for a multi-level spinal fusion procedure done from a posterior approach. If you could imagine the patient would end up with a vertical incision scar over their spine like a small zipper. At the time, spinal fusion technology had evolved, creating new procedures that with the right expertise, achieved great outcomes for the patient.

The posterior approach was a well-trodden path for a spinal surgeon. It was a traditional technique and as effective as a spinal fusion could be at the time. As a medical device representative, you could feel pretty confident that with a posterior fusion booking, the case would run reasonably smoothly, albeit at times – very, very slowly. (Two hours if we were lucky; up to six hours if not so lucky)

For this particular case, the surgeon phoned the evening before the surgery. It was 6pm on a Friday and I had just poured a glass of Chablis. I assumed our case would be cancelled. I was wrong.

"Peta, I am changing the operation on tomorrow's patient," he said.

"OK, what are you changing it to?" I asked.

"A lateral fusion" he replied.

Peta Sitcheff

A lateral fusion is a minimally invasive procedure performed with the patient on their side. The surgeon accesses the patient's spine through the side of their abdomen between the rib and the hip bone. A long cylindrical port providing access for specially designed angled instruments is used to prepare the space, place the interbody implant and complete the procedure. It is a procedure designed to minimise tissue destruction and facilitate quicker recovery. Like all procedures though, it isn't without its complexities. Minimally invasive surgery comes at a compromise - the surgeon's visual cues. In a posterior approach, the incision is large, and they can directly eyeball the critical structures to avoid. These structures act as land marks for prosthesis placement. In a lateral approach they rely on X-ray and neural monitoring to safely access the spine. Lateral cases have a steep learning curve. They generally go really well, but if they are difficult, they can go very poorly, very quickly. For a young, inexperienced surgeon without a senior watchful eye, it is tiger country.

Back to my young masked spinal surgeon. Less than 12 months into a consultancy, this surgeon threw himself into private practice. Unable to get his own regular operating time, the hospital would tag his cases onto another surgeon's list. Once the original surgeon's list had finished, he would "follow on" - generally after hours. As his representative, I often found myself starting complex cases at 9pm at night when most people would be tucking themselves up into bed. Finishing well after midnight, it was hard to see how that could set anyone up for success. Especially the patient.

This surgeon was notoriously indecisive. It wasn't unusual for him to change his surgical plan minutes before a case, but a lateral fusion wasn't so clear cut. This was a complex procedure, requiring totally different equipment, that when not performed by an experienced technician, could have catastrophic results.

At the time, there was no protocol requiring a surgeon to be formally accredited by the hospital to do the procedure. In spinal surgery, the use of new technology was not a regulated process. The approval of its use was monitored by the medical device companies. The same ones who benefited commercially from the sale.

I was intrigued.

> I know he has assisted a few of the senior guys, but I don't think he has been formally trained. Certainly not by us.

"OK, have you completed any official training for lateral fusion?" I queried.

"Oh no, I'm comfortable. I've assisted enough cases." he replied.

Here I was, being asked to send in surgical equipment for a complex case by a surgeon who I knew wasn't trained in the procedure, for a case less than 24 hours away. My brain went into overdrive.

> I'll need to call the warehouse, hope the equipment is there and not interstate. Hospital staff will have to be called in and paid overtime to process it for an 8am start tomorrow. I'll have to cover the case instead of my clinical who's on-call as this guy never listens at the best of times. I can't put her in that position. Christ, I'll need a babysitter too.

Then I backed up.

> What the hell am I thinking?

Forget the logistical nightmare and a potential sleepless night ahead, what I couldn't get past, was that this surgeon was willing to operate on a patient the next morning, doing a procedure he had not been properly trained to do. Rather, he would adopt the "see one, assist one, do one" method. I couldn't help but wonder how the patient and their family felt about the sudden change in plan. Putting their full faith in their surgeon, I guessed they would be none the wiser.

Nothing about this was sitting well. This wasn't the way I worked or a position I was comfortable putting myself in. Not one part of this last-minute decision change felt fair on anyone who would be in that room. Least of all the patient. If the shit hit the fan during the surgery, we would all be a part of the salvage and somehow, that felt inevitable.

  I don't want this work.

"I'm sorry," I replied. "I'm not willing to do this."

"I'll be fine so long as you come and cover the case," he said.

  Oh great. No pressure.

"Have you got anyone helping you?" I asked, thinking he might have invited a senior surgeon to assist.

"No, I am doing it."

  For the love of god.

I was horrified by his overzealous confidence. I was always so proud of our team and the way we conducted ourselves. It wasn't so much about what we did, it was more what we didn't do that was noticed in the industry. We didn't buy business, we respected ourselves and treated everyone equally.

We didn't want to be good at what we did, we wanted to be great.

In the absence of new technology as a market differentiator, for a long while, our reputation was all we had.

"I'm sorry, I'm not willing to put myself in the position of carrying you through

My Beautiful Mess

a case you are not properly trained in. It's not how we roll," I reinforced.

"Well if you don't want the sale, I'll ring your competitor. They are always there when I need them," he spat.

Ouch.

"Go for it. I really hope you get the outcome for the patient you are looking for," I replied.

He abruptly hung up and I suddenly felt very happy to have my Saturday morning back.

Arsehole.

Unfortunately for the patient, the case didn't go according to plan. A senior surgeon was called in to salvage the procedure and eventually, they reverted back to the original operation. The patient was put through an experience that could have been avoided.

It should not be up to a medical device representative who financially benefits from the use of their equipment to tell a surgeon whether they can or cannot conduct a procedure. However, in the absence of a formal accreditation process for spinal surgery by the hospital, at the time, there were few other filters.

Medical device companies will continue to provide equipment because rarely are they told they can't. All the while a consumer and rightly so, places all of their trust in their surgeon under the impression they are accessing the highest quality of care because of the high private insurance premiums they maintain. As a patient, I did, but I had the benefit of knowing the system.

The problem for others, they don't know what they don't know.

Recommended Reading
-

The Trusted Advisor
David H. Maister, Charles H. Green & Robert M. Galford
Published by Free Press (2000)

Applied Empathy
"The New Language of Leadership"
Michael Ventura
Published by Hodder & Stoughton (2019)

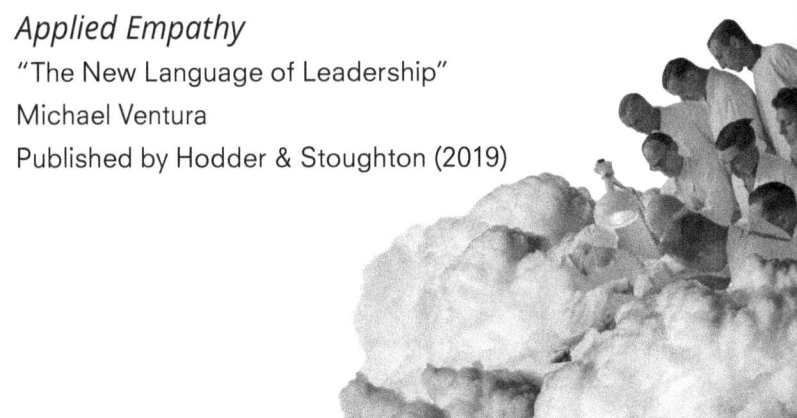

My Beautiful Mess

Peta Sitcheff

Managing the Beast
—

"Failing well is the hallmark of resilience"

Richard de Crespigny

Those early days on the road I didn't know if I felt like a kid in a candy store or a rabbit in head lights. Maybe a rabbit in a candy store! It took time, but as the months and years rolled by, I soon realised I was going to need the patience of Jobe to tolerate the long sales cycle that comes with unpacking and influencing the complex mind of a surgeon.

When the penny finally dropped that the smartest thing I could do was to focus on understanding my customers rather than myself, I settled in for the ride. Rather than worrying about winning or losing, I found success in the simplest gestures that didn't make anyone any money.

Being recognised by a passing masked spinal surgeon in the hospital corridor pepped my dragging feet into a springy step. Being offered their mobile number was like being given the key to a locked door of opportunity - access!

The first time a surgeon rang me on my mobile phone you could have knocked me over with a feather. I remember looking at his name in disbelief and being too frozen in shock to pick it up and answer the damn thing.

> Crap, what does he want? What will I say? How will I know what to say?

He was the first surgeon who ever booked my equipment for a surgery. I'll never forget it. I felt like I had conquered the world. I could do this. He was one of the most respectful and kindest neurosurgeons I ever worked with. He was the first person who took a chance on me and I am grateful we are still close enough friends today that I can remind him of that.

He gave me faith that my slow and steady focus, was the right path for me. I didn't need to be anyone I wasn't.

For years, the business flourished, and I flourished within it. Sales targets were smashed, my results handsomely rewarded, and my wins celebrated at sales conferences that had all of the gusto you could imagine a successful American company with a healthy ego could create. Bright lights, loud music, smile for the camera. We might have worked hard, but we played hard too.

My ego lapped it up, so much so I didn't recognise the dependency it was creating. I was becoming swept up in a viscous cycle, needing to win to feel successful and because work was all encompassing, that wasn't only successful at work, but successful in life.

I was accepting every surgery booking I could, running from hospital to hospital, trying to service the cases myself rather than delegating them out to the team.

Peta Sitcheff

You need to keep control Peta. Trust no one.

Like a diligent student, I would jump right on, holding that line white knuckle tight. I failed to realise that by not delegating and offering my trust to the team, I was sabotaging the likelihood of ever receiving any in return.

The masked surgeons aren't forgiving. If I'm not there, they will think I don't care. I can't let them down.

The days my mobile phone rang incessantly made me feel on top of the world. Each call, a shot of adrenalin that made me feel needed. I loved the sound of that ping, wished for it even. All of that hard work and patience was paying off. The bookings were coming, fast. A little too fast. Timeslots were being double booked, triple booked, some days, we had 10 surgeries to juggle. 10 kits of equipment, 10 surgeries needing someone in the room, 10 timetables changing with the demands of the day and 10 surgeons wanting equal attention.

There was one of me, only three in our team and 24 hours in a day.

Be careful what you wish for.

The Director's words from my job interview rang in my ears as I looked at a busy Thursday in the diary wondering how the heck I was going to manage it.

I'd do the best I could, making decisions based on the information I had at the time, contingency planning for as many possible scenarios my anxious brain could concoct. Just as I thought I had a handle of it all, another worse-case scenario thought storm would whip up in my brain like a sudden severe weather pattern. In this instance, it was a bloody god send - being able to sniff out risk was pretty damn useful when the stakes were high.

Maybe we really are a team? If I want to maintain control I have to stay ahead of the game. I need to anticipate every move and make

My Beautiful Mess

sure there's no unwanted surprises. Least of all for the surgeons.

Managing expectations was the saviour to my sanity. I learnt it was much more pleasant to juggle a circus act of expectations, than it was to deal with the atomic consequences of dishing something up to a masked surgeon they weren't prepared for.

I was yet to meet a surgeon who appreciated any surprise, least of all an unwanted one. Sending a colleague they didn't know, to cover a case without advance notice, had the potential to set everyone up for a rough day. My colleague's competence was rarely in question, it was more that if I did so, I was forcing the surgeon to work with someone they didn't know and trust. Regardless of how thorough the handover, I constantly felt I was letting them down.

It was a tough predicament to avoid as the business grew.

Overnight, it felt like I went from running a suburban hobby farm to a monstrous global export cattle station, with the flurry of logistical activity to match. I had equipment kits flying all over Australia, passing each other in the night sky as I tried to keep up with demand.

There were days I just drowned in decisions. Overwhelmed by the volume of information I was processing, petrified I would succumb to the perfectly normal human tendency of forgetting. Overlooking the smallest detail could have seismic consequences particularly when there was a patient involved.

"I'll have a six and a half by 50mm monoaxial screw" a masked surgeon said during a case. I froze in my tracks.

"Sorry doctor, did you say monoaxial?" I asked.

"Yes, I always use mono's in trauma cases." He replied in a tone that screamed "surely you know this" as the nursing staff scrambled to see what other sterile systems they had on hand.

I didn't send the monoaxial screws.

In my naivety, I hadn't even thought to ask. Needless to say, that early misstep tainted my reputation with that surgeon for my entire career.

"I don't think she has what it takes," he told a senior colleague of mine early on.

When someone in the logistical team who I was relying on to perform, disagreed, or pushed back on my requests, I felt the anger start to boil inside of me.

"Please make this easy. Don't tell me we can't," I pleaded.

It was 9pm at night and I was ringing each of the hospitals for the surgeries scheduled the next day. I knew if I made this the one time I didn't call, it would be the one time something would go wrong.

"Has the equipment arrived?", "Is it sterilised?", "You only have 6 of the 7 crates?", "OK. I'll follow up with the warehouse."

They had left one behind on the loading dock.

"Please expect an extra crate tonight. It's expected to arrive close to midnight and will need to be sterilised straight away for the 8am surgery. I'm so sorry," I said.

"Has there been any change to the surgery list order?", "Yes? It's now first not third on the list?"

Crap.

My Beautiful Mess

I pick up the phone and ring a colleague in Sydney to jump on a 6am flight to help us out. Four surgeries at 8am and only three of us. The numbers said it all.

> Where will I go? Whichever one I choose to attend there'll be relief there and judgement where I am not. I will use the "patient first" as my house rule. No surgeon can argue if the patient is at the centre of my decision. I'll send myself to service the surgery where the patient has the greatest risk. The less experienced surgeon doing the complex case. The surgery with the most moving parts. That is where I need to be.

I stumbled into bed around 11pm. My muscles were drained of energy, but my mind wide was awake. Like a newborn who couldn't yet tell night from day.

> There's so much that can go wrong tomorrow. So much.

I would almost drift off and then my brain would be like a bull poked with a burning hot cattle prod. As the minutes then hours passed, the more anxious I became about not sleeping.

> I need to sleep. I must remember to turn that tray around for sterilization quickly. I can't forget to check the 6.5 x 45mm screw quantity. Hopefully, that box arrived. Crap, I forgot to check today.

I spent most of the night tossing and turning in one of those dozy half sleep states. All night I had crazy dreams, wild stories full of muddled facts from all parts of my life. As the alarm went off, my brain would fill with the logistics of the monstrous workload ahead. All I wanted to do was pull the doona up around my ears and settle into a dreamy slumber.

> That's alright. I'll sleep tonight.

Peta Sitcheff

It was hard not to wish those days away.

Recommended Reading
-

The Checklist
"How to get things right"
Atul Gawande
Published by Profile Books Ltd (2011)

The Art of Quiet Influence
"Timeless Wisdom for Leading Without Authority"
Jocelyn Davis
Published by Nicholas
Brealey Publishing (2019)

My Beautiful Mess

Peta Sitcheff

Boundaries
—

"The only people who get upset about you having boundaries are the ones who are benefiting from you having none." Anon

With competitors nipping at my heels, the behaviour of the masked spinal surgeons evolved to reflect the changing landscape. Darwin's theory really could be applied to all species. For years I'd clambered with the best in the market to grow my business and suddenly, I was faced with losing it. It was unfamiliar, unsettling and came with a flare of unexpected emotions.

Winning the business of a masked spinal surgeon was like winning the lottery. I kept investing time in the relationship each week, never sure when I would hit the jackpot. They were complex creatures of habit for a reason. Change introduced risk and when the stakes were high, you had to have a pretty good reason to ride the wave of disruption change would bring. As a sales professional you looked for that "gap" or reason to switch. The weakest link in the competitor's offering that you could amplify, to start concocting

My Beautiful Mess

the case for change.

I distinctly remember my first call where that opportunity came. I had a three-day old baby.

Back then there was no government funded or company paid maternity leave in the business. I did everything I could to hide my pregnancy for as long as I could. I was petrified that if the competitors got wind I was taking time off, they would swoop in and attack my business and all that would be left when I returned would be a dead smelly carcass. All of that hard work undone in an instant. In hindsight, I should have had more faith in the strength of my customer relationships.

Fortunately, surgical scrubs are made for comfort just like an oversized pair of flannel pyjamas. I managed to discreetly hide my bump until I was 21 weeks before anyone in the market knew. It was as though it happened overnight. At 19 weeks into the pregnancy I woke up early one morning in tremendous abdominal pain.

> Gas? No. I can't fart this pain away.

Instinctively, I knew the baby was fine and that this had something to do with me. The pain was deep and intensifying by the minute. I made a 6am trip to the local public hospital emergency department, thankful to have had the foresight to ring the obstetrician and keep him in the loop with what was going on. As I was whisked by an ambulance to the private hospital in the city, the ER doctor's parting words sank in:

"I won't let you have that operation in this hospital."

Four hours later I was "sans appendix", thankful at the time it couldn't grow back.

Being pregnant, I'd had an open rather than keyhole procedure and refused

Peta Sitcheff

post-operative pain relief thinking my kiddo had probably done enough tripping around inside of me, courtesy of the general anaesthetic. I chose instead to lie very, very still for seven days in an obstetrics ward amongst the new mums and screaming babies. I couldn't have made myself more miserable if I'd tried. 10 days after the surgery I was straight back to work. It was too early, but I didn't want to take any more time off. In three years I had barely taken one sick day off, let alone 10 days in a row.

The way my body grew, I didn't have much of a belly, pre-appendix. However, when I went back to work post-surgery, my belly had popped. Given no one knew about the pregnancy, it was like I had two weeks off, a baby implanted, and my appendectomy was jokingly questioned. Needless to say, learning I was 22 weeks pregnant certainly surprised a few.

When my still nameless bub was three days old, I had a call from The Director. I could hear a flicker of emotion, almost desperation in his usually controlled, articulate voice.

"Sorry to bother you, I need help," he started

"Sure, what's up?" I said.

"We have received a call from a masked spinal surgeon, he has fired his supplier and would like all of our equipment in his office at 3pm."

It was now 11am.

"What the fuck? Pardon my language!" I responded.

"I'm going to need to come in and get a debrief from you on how to handle this," he said.

> I've been calling on this guy for 3 years and now, after 3 weeks off with a three day old baby, he throws us an opportunity? Could he

My Beautiful Mess

have picked worse timing? He could have picked any number of companies, but he chose us. Yes! This is what I've been working so hard for. Christ almighty. I can't miss this opportunity.

I could feel my brain running away from me with excitement as I lay there with icicle packs between my legs numbing my wounds. This was enormous. I glanced down at myself.

> Somehow, I don't think the surgeon is going to appreciate me turning up direct from the hospital, pale from blood loss, antibiotics dripping into my arm. Don't be stupid!

I had to rely on The Director and a temporary replacement who was trying to fill my shoes and hated the job, to hold the fort. While I waited for him to show, my brain went into overdrive.

> Could they do as good a job as I could? Why was this happening now? I have done a stack of work to get this customer to this point and I'm not even going to be there to reap the reward. I've been waiting three years for an opportunity like this. Bloody hell. I'll just have to do what I can to help them set it up and hope like hell he's still working with us when I come back in a few months. I wasn't planning on being off for long...

There I was in hospital, with my three day old baby, sitting on my icicles. You could have fried an egg from the heat radiating off my boobs as they filled with milk. The Director entered a short while later in his suit and tie and sat stiffly in a vinyl covered chair, next to my brand new baby boy.

I rapidly dictated account onboarding instructions from my hospital bed. We were still going as the nurse came in to help me with a feed, raising her eyebrows as she overheard our conversation. As my boobs came out, his eyes fled straight to the wall behind me.

Peta Sitcheff

"Poor bugger, how awkward" I thought, amused by his awkwardness as I tried to explain the personality of said masked spinal surgeon over the loud snuffles of my ravenous newborn.

I must have had rocks in my head, but it was my choice. I was determined to have input, such was the importance I placed on myself. That surgeon was clear of his intent upfront, our hourglass would run for three months to "teach his previous supplier a lesson" (which turned out to be a political one).

I would likely miss that boat, as that was when I was meant to be returning to work. The horse was galloping, my brain jumping ahead.

What if we could hang onto that business for longer?

Somehow, with the oldest and clunkiest equipment, we hung onto that business for 10 years and to this day he continues to be not only a great friend, but also my own surgeon.

I gripped my business tightly. All of us in the industry did.

It was hard to gain and could be lost in a heartbeat. When a customer "played the field" it hurt.

One of my largest customers had been working with me for ten years. I'd worked with him since his first year out of training, enduring the long hours as he slugged through his first instrumented cases. I always made myself available to work the afterhours – the only time he was given lists by the hospital. I'd been as attentive as I knew how, to deliver what he needed to get the job done, never skipping a beat. His business was worth more than $1 million dollars a year.

When he began "playing the field" it was unnerving. Actually, it felt like a kick in the guts.

My Beautiful Mess

>You're not good enough! He is bored with you.

My mind would clutch onto the hook that had been thrown, and the obsessing would start. The horse would bolt as my assumptions would run wild.

>He always hated that torque wrench. If only I could have fixed it sooner.
>
>Maybe I said something wrong?
>
>Maybe I did something wrong?
>
>If only I was at his last case, maybe I could have stopped this from happening?

Fictional stories made up of guess work would swirl around my brain until I knew his justification for changing suppliers. Usually, there was a perfectly rational reason for the switch.

"Oh, the patient already had the competitor hardware in place. We were extending a level," he would casually slip into conversation.

>Bloody hell. Don't you know what you've put me through?
>
>It is bloody annoying when you cheat on me, don't you know how much I've given up to do this job well. Stop mucking with my head and making me feel like I'm not good enough at what I do!

It was an emotional wave I had to ride out. I had to go with the flow and hope the surgeon would circle back, which most of the time, they did. Particularly when the stakes were high for the patient and it really mattered. They were the times you were reminded you were valued. That who you were and what you offered was enough.

Peta Sitcheff

Even if those moments were on Christmas morning.

In our house, Christmas resembled a perfect festive snow globe, full of colourful happiness shared with my favourite loves in the whole world. At 45, it still makes me feel like a big kid. The sound of Lewis creeping down the stairs to see if his Santa sack is full (you have to believe to receive in our house), the cyclone of brightly coloured wrapping paper above our heads as it is torn off in a frenzy by Lewis and his younger cousins, their hyperactive squeals and beaming smiles filling the room with joy. There are copious cuddles of thanks, while the Pogues slur "Fairytale in New York" in the background on the airwaves. All the while the aroma of Mum's roasting pork loin builds in intensity, filling every room in the house, teasing our tummies.

I wouldn't trade it for quids and detest when it is interrupted.

Spinal surgery patients don't take public holidays, especially in the summer when the alcohol is flowing, water is beckoning, and stupidity prevails. The influx of broken backs filling operating rooms during Melbourne's 40°C hot spells was inevitable over summer. In fact, we'd often leave the equipment in the hospitals with extra stock during December because we knew there would be plenty of instances of people jumping off a jetty into a river and well, missing the river. It was tragic, but unfortunately it was also a reality.

Work had invaded many a Christmas morning in my household and this one, was no different.

Amongst the carols and chaos, was the undeniable ping of my mobile phone. If only it were a friend wishing us Christmas greetings.

> No, no, no! Not now dammit.

Not wanting to pull my family out of their happiness bubble, I very discreetly went to "check on the pork" roasting in the oven. I didn't want to be distracted that Christmas morning and until I did something about it, I knew I would be.

My Beautiful Mess

Assuming the worst, I started preparing my brain for a day in the operating room, all the while praying for divine intervention.

>Please no, please no, please no.

I listened to the voicemail.

"I have a complex case to discuss with you on a patient with dwarfism," he said.

My heart sank.

>Oh Christ, it isn't even straight forward!

In the past I would have instantly hit redial, but this time I thought better of it. Thinking of what was enough. I didn't want to have to speak to him so I sent the surgeon a text acknowledging his message.

"Sounds like an interesting case. What is your time frame? Let me know when suits you to discuss?" I typed.

"Oh. It's not urgent, you didn't need to respond. I won't be doing the surgery until the end of January. I just didn't want to forget to tell you. Have a great Christmas with Lewis," he responded instantly.

>Oh, for the love of god!

For whatever reason, on that Christmas morning, the surgeon needed to let me know about a surgery that was a month away. He couldn't have known the visceral reaction it would provoke within me. There was no sense that it was a holiday, Christmas or that I might be with my family. He just didn't want to forget.

I had assumed the case was urgent. I assumed he needed a response.

Peta Sitcheff

I assumed if I didn't acknowledge the message I would lose the case to the competition.

That was my last Christmas in the job.

I shudder now when I think of how often I prioritised my customers over family.

In the era of no paid maternity leave, my six months maternity leave fast turned into three and with the new account having dropped whilst I was on leave, my replacement was a flight risk. I couldn't blame her. A massive increase in workload and a new masked personality to manage, this wasn't a work environment she was ready to embrace or a situation she was willing to put up with for long. She wanted out of there and was already one sneaker-clad foot out the door.

Lewis was seven weeks old. I couldn't sit down properly due to lingering pain from the trauma. I was still breast feeding and he was waking in the middle of the night for a feed. That lasted about three weeks. There was no way I could continue breast feeding on a surgery schedule. It was too unreliable. I couldn't leave a surgery to pump milk if we were in the middle of instrumenting. "Sorry doctor, please excuse me while I pump my boobs," didn't quite feel right in an operating room, nor did the sight of leaky nipples through surgical scrubs. Dragging a pump around hospital to hospital would be a pain in the arse and I would need an esky to store the milk in. Too hard. Tough love was required. With that, my husband Troy and I, changed his menu to powdered formula and donned our hard hats, ready for a night of controlled crying. The first night, endless crying echoed up the halls. There we lay, in the darkened early hours of the morning, torturing ourselves by not relenting to Lewis's hunger fuelled screams. What was 40 minutes, felt like hours. The second night, 10 minutes. The third night, we woke up startled at 5.30am, racing to check he was still alive in his cot. We hadn't heard a peep from his room all night.

My Beautiful Mess

There he was, wide awake in the shadows, his chubby little face beaming with pride for himself. He had done it! Squeals of delight from him, relieved laughter from us. Thank goodness he delivered, I had no idea how I would have done the working parent thing otherwise.

Returning to work did offer one unexpected reprieve.

The masked surgeons seemed to understand the new lens I was peering through and the conflicting responsibilities that were grappling for my attention. They seemed to understand and accept it better than I did.

I don't know why this came as such a surprise. It was as though I had forgotten many of them were parents themselves. Rather than "talking shop" in the tea room, I now found myself trading stories about wild nights with newborns and listening to undiscovered chapters of surgeons lives. Whether I had never been interested in the past, or I had just thought they wouldn't want to talk about it, I'm not sure. It was as though I now had permission to loosen up and show the odd blemish, but that didn't sit so easily with me.

I didn't have an instruction manual on how to loosen the reins on the business. I needed to control its every moving part to feel in control of myself. It was the only way I knew how to manage the beast it had become.

Now, I had this beautiful, gentle natured, chubby little being, competing for my attention. Attention that had always been reserved for my surgeons. I had spent years trying to crack the codes of their personalities and influence their thoughts. They were responsible for my family's livelihood and able to unwittingly manipulate my self-worth with the decisions they made. All because I let them.

I needed that lucrative return. It made me feel like I mattered.

Now, I was trying to stay in control of a business the way I always had, while my heart strings were being pulled towards home. Rather than give in, an

Peta Sitcheff

emotional tug-o-war started brewing inside of me as I desperately tried not to let anyone down. I found myself making compromises. Each one digging a little deeper into my conscience. Leaving a surgery little earlier than I should, not flying across town to do an extra check on equipment for a big case the next day, justifying a rare free afternoon at home instead of being out there amongst the surgeons or having someone cover a case to give me a reprieve. I had never given myself a reprieve. That would mean not being in control.

I had to keep going. This was my life. I needed this job to survive and now I was a Mum, I had to make it work. It was a hopeless situation.

Every exhausted step on the treadmill started numbing me of emotion. The robot within me kicked in, as I box ticked my way through a day. I wanted to collapse as soon as I got home. Instead, I was inventing mashed vegetable concoctions, racing for nappies before the "5 minutes until closing" call, finding missing dummies under the couch and stepping in dog poo as I hung the washing on the line in the dark. All to do it again, the next day.

With the drawn-out grieving process for my father playing out in parallel to my working parent existence, I gradually became a hollowed-out version of myself. An expressionless walking shell with no insides. It was as though my feelings had been scooped out and replaced with, nothing. There was simply nothing.

"There was a name for this?" I remember thinking, as Troy and I sat in the GP clinic listening to her words. Those two words "postnatal depression" offered the glimmer of hope we both needed to feel we could get through this.

That I could be fixed.

Unfortunately, it wouldn't be without casualties. I had crippled my ability to connect with people costing me not only friendships, but my marriage.

Recommended Reading

-

Lost Connections
"Uncovering the Real Causes of Depression and the Unexpected Solutions"
Johann Hari
Published by Bloomsbury Publishing (2018)

Option B
"Facing Adversity, Building Resilience and Finding Joy"
Sheryl Sandberg & Adam Grant
Published by Penguin Random House UK (2017)

Peta Sitcheff

Grief
-

"They say you die twice. One time when you stop breathing and a second time, a bit later on, when someone says your name for the last time"
Banksy

"How will I know?" I whispered to the nurse unit manager of the palliative care ward. My voice wobbled with meek trepidation. I was petrified for his response but secretly hoping this bubble it felt we were in wouldn't last much longer. It felt like time was standing still.

I have never in my life been more present than in those hours. I was oblivious to any life outside of those four hospital walls. The past no longer mattered, as for the future, even tomorrow seemed too far away for now. I cared about nothing but the here and now.

Each of my senses were hyper alert, drinking in every detail of their surrounds as they engraved their memory on my brain forever. The clanging plates on

My Beautiful Mess

the kitchen trolley as it rolled over a join in the floor, the whimpering of a grieving family member in the lounge, the stale smell of unbathed skin and acidotic breath, the dry, bland taste of black Lipton's tea, the discomfort of the hard, vinyl lounge chair I slept in overnight. I remember it all as though it was yesterday, not 13 years ago and despite the harshness in the tone of these words, at the time I felt strangely safe and nurtured amongst those walls.

I had never experienced death like it before, it was prolonged and imminent. Behind every door in the dimly lit ward, was an experience similar to ours and a life about to expire. The hospital staff were remarkable, knowing exactly what to do, what to say and when to say it. How they did it, day in and day out was beyond me. They understood and respected the extreme intimacy of what we were experiencing and balanced it beautifully with their clinical duties in discretely keeping Dad as comfortable as possible.

As for my emotions, they were in unchartered territory. It was like they were navigating a foreign, tumultuous terrain towards an expected destination, but they were totally unaware how long it would take or what the journey would be like. Maybe it was a bit like when man first landed on the moon?

As for answering "how will I know?" the nurse unit manager was right, I knew immediately. I hadn't been out of his room for more than 20 minutes, long enough to escape the palliative "bubble" and walk the long desolate corridor to the deserted hospital cafeteria on the floor below. I grabbed a plastic triangle of egg and lettuce sandwich, partially stale from refrigeration, and headed back to the ward.

I ate while I walked but could only manage a few bites. The overhanging smell of death and disinfectant robbing me of my hunger. As I turned to walk through the doorway to Dad's room, I stopped, frozen by what I saw. He had changed. In my 20 minute absence, Dad's lips had turned blue and his face, a shade of grey I will never in my life forget. It was a hue resigned only for those whose beating hearts were slowing to a gradual standstill.

Peta Sitcheff

He was alone. His raspy, forced breaths all that could be heard in the dimly lit room, the silence interrupted by my shrill yelp, "Help!" With that, my step mother Helen, came running into the room followed by the nurse unit manager who looked at our ashen faces and solemnly nodded. We understood, it was time.

I could taste the egg and lettuce sandwich climbing up my throat as I swallowed heavily to keep it from reappearing in a regurgitative state. These were the last moments I would ever see my father alive. Together, his wife and I sat by his side, holding his hand, stroking his brow and letting him know it was OK to let go. He no longer needed to suffer through the pain, to pretend he was OK when he clearly wasn't. He no longer needed to be brave. As the minutes ticked by, his body started heaving with each raspy breath. As they became shorter and shallower, Helen and I exchanged glances, both wondering each time if it would be his last. Just when we thought it was the end, he heaved an enormous breath, as though he had burst through the ocean surface after a long, deep-sea dive.

Then, there was nothing. No sound. No movement. Just perfect stillness, as he let go of his 61 years. His spirit floating gracefully above us, towards the next chapter of his being as an eagle. He always wanted to come back as an eagle.

Compared to many, Dad's cancer journey was reasonably short.

386 days to be exact. The days stood next to each other like book spines on a shelf, each representing a chapter of his cancer tale, perfectly bookended in time by the weddings of his daughters.

Yep. Dad's timing was uncanny.

I cast my mind back to the moment he walked me, his eldest daughter, down the aisle. I am forever grateful he had the opportunity to experience his

My Beautiful Mess

moment as the proud "father of the bride" and often think of it as the day he walked both of his daughters down the aisle, even if at the time, none of us realised it.

For those not in the know, Victoria dishes up two types of Easter weekend. They are either, beautiful Autumn days, where the sun's warm rays reflect brilliant amber hues, the warmth against your skin is like a warm, comforting hug. It is glorious. We had the second type of Easter weekend on our wedding day in Daylesford - a blisteringly cold afternoon, with a blast chill from the south pole that must have knocked at least 10 degrees off the Bureau's recorded temperature.

Dad arrived to fulfil his duty of collecting the bride. He looked puffy and bloated, his newly purchased linen sports jacket pulling at the button, tight across his tummy. He must have been feeling awful on the inside, but probably not wanting to detract from the celebrations, didn't utter a word. Instead he held his head high in pride, smiling ear to ear as I took his arm and together we strolled down the red carpet towards the outdoor alter. We laughed the whole way, as the teeth of our guests chattered around us and the wind whipped my chiffon train into the air like a silk tornado. My bridesmaids fought against the wind, desperately trying to hold their silk dresses down, preventing the broadcasting of their knickers to the world. The poor loves were frozen to the bone. Everyone was, except me that is. I had my 24 week bun baking in my oven keeping me toasty and reminding me with a fluttery kick every once and while that he was there for the fun too. I remember in that moment, saying a few prayers of gratitude for those fluttery kicks, considering the recent trauma of the appendectomy.

Once we retreated to the cosy, woodfired warmth of the restaurant, the evening proceeded beautifully. The corks popped, the carefully selected wine flowed, the rustic banquet stacked the tables as Moroccan aromas of harissa and slow cooked lamb filled the room. The quirky local DJ was in the corner. His vinyls pumped out the old time tunes. It was more than a worthy celebration of two families and their friends united.

Peta Sitcheff

Having had a good crack at the celebration, Dad retired early and was already looking forward to the "morning after" BBQ lunch planned the following day, particularly my father-in-law's homemade, spicy, Italian chorizo sausages. Dad loved his food and the next day, Freddie, well known for his charcuterie delicacies, was running the show.

Overnight, Dad's health took a serious nosedive. Within 24 hours he was sent to Emergency at Ballarat hospital where he was diagnosed with a significant sized bowel obstruction fully occluding his personal plumbing causing him to be violently ill. The obstruction was removed, along with a significant portion of his bowel, the surgery revealing an advanced malignant tumour that the doctors suspected wasn't a lone soldier. They were right. The cancer was everywhere. His bowel, liver, lungs to start.

On the insistence of family, Troy and I had started on our honeymoon trek to the beautiful McLaren Vale. We were all trying to be optimistic, but deep down I think we knew this wasn't going to end well. As the situation unravelled and information started filtering through, after 24 hours we did a swift U-turn and headed straight to Ballarat ICU.

I remember feeling like I was having an out of body experience. We were parking a car full of wedding joy – gifts, mementos and clothes in the car park of the hospital, to go and see Dad in the ICU. It was like being flung by a slingshot from joy to hell in a heartbeat.

From the crisp, icy cold Ballarat day we walked into the tropical warmth of the ICU. The thick air made me feel claustrophobic, as unwelcome memories of nauseating morning sickness started to overcome me.

Dad's face was pale and yellow, the fluorescent lights above him accentuating the dark shadows under his eyes. His stapled surgical scar like a long zipper up his abdomen. I remember thinking to myself, "if he coughs, will it split open?". It looked so painful. As he opened his eyes, they filled with tears at

My Beautiful Mess

the sight of us standing there.

"I'm in a bit of trouble Pete," he whispered as they closed, and he drifted off into a drug induced slumber.

Dad arrived in Victoria from Queensland as father-of-the bride, as excited as a kid in a candy store for the five days of festivities ahead. He didn't treat himself to new clothes often, but he couldn't wait for this weekend to model his brand-new threads, carefully chosen by him to compliment my gown and show case his individual style. No one could ever tell Dad what to wear or what to do for that matter, he was one of a kind and desperately wanted to make his daughters proud.

Instead of the expected five day long celebrations, Dad left Victoria after three weeks as a Stage 4 cancer patient. For three weeks, my sister and I trekked the road from Melbourne to Ballarat after work to be with him while we could. One week turned to two, then morphed into three. I had gone from 24 weeks to 27 weeks pregnant and was starting to wonder if Dad would ever see his first born grandchild.

The day he left hospital to return home to the Sunshine Coast was a carefully orchestrated exercise between family, doctors, airlines and ambulance services. I'll never forget the moment he emerged from the automatic hospital doors. As they opened, he was wheeled out by a nurse wearing the biggest smile, just like he did when he walked me down the aisle. He was a shadow of his former self, 15 kilograms lighter than when he arrived and swimming in tracksuit fabric as the fleecy cotton swamped his frame.

The expression of relief on his face was his brightest fashion accessory that day.

"What will this cancer journey mean?" I wondered. The autumn trees whizzed past on the roadside as we drove to the airport. None of us knew. We had been told it was aggressive, but how did that translate to prognosis – 3

Peta Sitcheff

months? 1 year? 3 years?

As he was wheeled by the manicured air hostess through the gate onto the plane, he turned and gave us a royal wave to rival the Queen's. We waved frantically back. I was smiling on the outside but petrified on the inside I might never see my Dad again.

The coming months were a blur. Work, new baby, Dad's chemotherapy updates. Repeat.

He wasn't well enough to fly to Melbourne when Lewis was born and after six weeks, I was well enough to make the journey with my new kiddo to Brisbane and introduce him to his grandfather. It had been four months and I hadn't seen Dad since that day we drove him to the airport. I remember thinking how excited he must have been feeling in anticipation of seeing us. I drove straight from Brisbane airport to the hospital where Dad was having chemo. Of all things, Steve Irwin's funeral was on the radio on the way in.

"Crikey, could the day get any more emotional?" I remember thinking in true crocodile hunter fashion.

Dad had told the nursing staff he was expecting us and clearly, they had succumbed to his charm. They all knew exactly who we were, welcoming us with huge smiles and couldn't wait to take us to where dad was having his dose of chemo. As we rounded the corner to see the long row of patient recliners, every set of eyes and smiling face nodded in Dad's direction. There he was.

With Lewis strapped to my front, Dad's eyes met mine with a look of what I can only describe as disbelief. It was like he couldn't quite believe we were actually there. The next moments were precious as Dad, overcome with emotion, marvelled at this little man in his arms who looked and still does, exactly like him.

My Beautiful Mess

I like to think we gave him an injection of life that day. While his body was being fed poisonous drugs, his heart was receiving a dose of love and his spirit was reminded that cancer had not totally overtaken his life.

He was loved.

There weren't too many months that passed before it was clear that Dad's cancer wasn't disappearing. It was difficult living in a different state and not being able to see him often. As much as he tried to tell us he was OK, you could tell he was protecting us from what his days were really like. As the weeks passed, you could sense he knew his time was running out. Before long, the time between his hospital stays became shorter as the stays themselves became longer.

He knew he didn't have long.

In the April 2007, my sister's wedding was weeks away and preparations were in full swing. I distinctly remember receiving a phone call from Dad. He was frantic.

"Did you get my email?" he asked.

"Huh?" I replied, oblivious to what he was talking about.

"I've sent you an email, let me know the minute you get it," he said forcefully.

"Alright, settle down!" I said as I wondered what on earth he was carrying on about.

I raced home to check my email, only to find a message with an attachment. It was his wedding speech for my sister Tina and her fiancé Oli's wedding.

My brain went straight to what he was trying to tell me.

Peta Sitcheff

"Come on Dad, you have to make it, 14 more days." I thought to myself. He knew he couldn't hold on much longer, but given we were in the middle of a whirlwind of silk and tulle, with preparations flurrying around us - what was I to do with this information? What was the right thing to do?

My plan of attack was to put my protective big sister hat on, sit on it and hope like hell it wouldn't be required.

Friends and family from far and wide embarked on the beachside town of Byron Bay the weekend before the Friday May 4th nuptials. The week was everything it should be, plenty of "togetherness", blissful wedding preparations and everyone drunk on love.

Then I received the phone call. It was like being struck by lightning, jolting me back to Dad's reality. It was Tuesday and Dad was being taken to emergency on the Sunshine Coast. By Wednesday he was being transferred to a hospital in Brisbane under the supervision of his Oncologist and it became clear he would be in hospital for the week. The wedding wasn't a part of that schedule.

Breaking the news to Tina and Oli was one of the toughest conversations I have ever had.

"I don't want our wedding to end up like yours," they both cried.

"It won't. You will have your day and it will be wonderful. First thing is first though, we need to go and see Dad in Brisbane, tonight. He will want to see you before the wedding," I said.

I picked them up late that Wednesday afternoon, both of them in the back seat, the atmosphere in the car thick with dread. Nobody spoke. A few minutes up the road I pulled over and turned around.

"I know this is absolutely shit and I have no idea what we are walking into, but we have to see him. We will spend some time and when you are ready, I will

My Beautiful Mess

drive you back to Byron Bay. Tomorrow morning, we will wake up in Byron and it will be all about you, it will be your day."

Pulling into the bottle shop drive thru for a couple of "travellers" we settled in for the two hour journey north. I've never been more grateful for that decision. Dad was delirious and seeing demons. Thankfully, he recognised us, albeit according to his chemically influenced brain, we were all lime green in colour.

It was the last time we saw him conscious. He fully thought he was going to make it to the wedding that Friday and we let him think so. It was a small but priceless gift we could all offer him in what would clearly be his last days. On May 4th, the force of Dad was with us. Tina and Oli married at *Rae's on Wategos*, a stunning beachside venue, and the celebration was as you would expect, wildly happy.

I proudly spoke for Dad that night, knowing my words would be forever remembered on this momentous day.

"There is one person who can't be here in person tonight, but guaranteed he is here in spirit," I started.

Grateful to Dad for always knowing best, I enlisted the help of a wonderful bridal party as we went on to lead the room in Dad's rendition of, *Always Look on the Bright Side of Life*. His dedication to Tina and Oli. Thank goodness I received that email.

Dad's spirit was so present that night. To this day, I will always wonder if that was the moment it left his body for good. It was time.

The following day as the "after party" was in full swing, the call came that Dad wouldn't make it through the night. Back on the road we went. We knew the way.

Peta Sitcheff

Lewis stayed with Mum in Byron Bay, my husband Troy drove the three of us to Brisbane to be with Dad. I was grateful to have him there.

Dad survived the night and as the sun rose, the decision was made for Troy to take Tina and Oli back to Byron. They had overseas guests with them and were leaving for their honeymoon the next morning. There wasn't any more we could do. It was up to Dad. He was leaving us.

Then he was gone.

I had been in the hospital for not quite 24 hours but it felt like days, weeks even. I felt like I was on another planet. As Dad lay there lifeless, we said our goodbyes. The nurse unit manager brought us his wedding ring in a clear, zip lock plastic bag and just like that, Helen grabbed his small overnight bag with now useless belongings and we walked out of the room.

As Helen's sister picked her up, I sat in the hospital foyer, reality setting in. My Dad was dead. I was in Brisbane and my family were in Byron Bay. I felt numb, like a zombie not in control of my body. It was my body not my brain that led me to a taxi and took me to the local bus depot. I sat there on the hard, green plastic chair, my non-blinking stare fixed on the digital arrivals and departures board. I wondered who these people were around me and then as the boarding notice echoed across the loud speaker, I alighted the bus and travelled to Byron Bay in a seat on my own.

My Beautiful Mess

Peta Sitcheff

Single Life
–

"The difference between shame and guilt is the difference between "I am bad" and "I did something bad"
Brené Brown

I quickly learnt if I was going to survive as a single working parent, I would have to learn to both rely on, and trust those around me. I now had a parenting roster to abide by and a four year old kiddo who needed both my mind and body in the one place at the same time.

The minute I tried to work while he was around, he would suddenly need something and demand my attention. It was like he just knew that for that minute, my mind had drifted to work, and my attention was elsewhere. He was letting me know that for him – it wasn't OK. If I was playing with him and a customer would ring, I had to check my phone. All of a sudden, he and my phone were competing for my attention. I wish I could say he won 100% of the time.

My Beautiful Mess

The hardest times were the weekends when I would be called for a surgery. If it was a weekend when I was on my own, it was fine. I welcomed the call. It made me feel needed when on the inside, I felt neglected. It curbed the loneliness and kept me quiet.

When surgery was scheduled on a parenting weekend, it sent me into turmoil. I hated having to ask for help. I'd be on the phone to a friend or to Troy to look after Lewis, disrupting their plans. He was used to early morning drop offs. Albeit you could see the confusion in his big brown eyes when I had him up at 7am on a weekend, "there is no school today Mum" he would say as I'd bundle him into the car in his PJ's. A one o'clock pick up, would be pushed out to two, three o'clock as unplanned delays or complications extended surgery time. As the minutes and hours ticked by, the tension on my heart strings strengthened until my chest hurt from the emotional pain.

It felt like I was being robbed of my mothering time. I wouldn't have a weekend with him for another two weeks. Resentment really was the poison of joy and it took everything in me to not wear the rising sensation on my face. My synthetic mask, and radio-opaque goggles acted as the perfect emotional camouflage.

Then there was the shame.

Beneath the superficial emotions, was a deeply buried layer of shame I tried desperately to ignore. Shame for the smidgeon of relief I felt when that surgery booking came through. Relief that once Lewis was dropped off, so too would be my parenting responsibilities. Time off from having to keep him occupied, trying to get him to fit into the disciplined structure I needed to feel like I could get through the day. Hours where I held on so tightly to my expectations for the day, that when they didn't go according to plan, I turned into a version of myself I didn't like very much. A rigid, cold, demanding version who needed control to cope.

Peta Sitcheff

What sort of mother are you? What sort of mother chooses work over being with their child? Someone who isn't a very good mother that's who.

Today's Reflection
-

When you work in a job where you are not in control of your own time, you make compromises. Often at the expense of your own well-being. Albeit initially, you might not realise that is the case. In an ideal world, it is up to your organisation to set you up for long term success, to recognise the pressure you are under and provide the resources you need to both sustain the distance and protect their business.

What they aren't responsible for is your personal self-preservation. Employers aren't mind readers. Your welfare is your responsibility and with that comes the necessity to lay personal boundaries that fiercely protect what is most valuable to your person.

If you are struggling, you have to tell them. If they don't listen, make them.

Recommended Reading
—

Daring Greatly
'How the Courage to be Vulnerable Transforms the Way We Live, Love, Parent and Lead'
Brené Brown
Published by Penguin Random House UK (2015)

Nine Lies About Work
Marcus Buckingham & Ashley Goodall
Published by Harvard Business Review Press (2019)

Peta Sitcheff

Fear
-

"Sooner or later, everyone sits down to a banquet of consequences"
Robert Louis Stevenson

As time passed, I was starting to feel like I was stuck on a highway, putting along in my old Cortina and the rest of my industry colleagues were whizzing past in their Ferraris. Even more perplexing, was a slow rising suspicion that I no longer felt I belonged.

Just keep to yourself. Everyone thinks you like it that way.

Ambitious colleagues I had worked with years ago were now impressively at the helm of companies. Those determined to raise bilingual children had embarked on exciting expat adventures overseas. Many friends had progressed into office-based roles with more family friendly hours and new intellectual challenges, while others were high flying executives. While they were running companies and travelling in Business Class, I was having the same conversations, with the same customers, wearing the same surgical

My Beautiful Mess

pyjamas and patent blue clogs.

The strongest life line that kept me from moving on, was the loyalty I had for my customers. After so many years, I couldn't bear the thought of disappointing them or perhaps more selfishly, how much my self-worth relied on their requests. I needed to feel needed.

I am ashamed to say now that at the time, I was more loyal to them than I was my own family. My personal world reflected a tumultuous weather pattern. I needed for one part of my life to remain constant and it was easier for that to be work.

Ironically, the cold, sterile operating room provided a warm, homely comfort.

The job was financially enabling. They may have gotten blood, but they paid handsomely for it. After my divorce when the opportunity presented itself to buy the family home outright, I jumped at it. I was none the wiser of how difficult it would prove to be. I scrimped and saved to add to the equity in the hope that the bank, any bank, would approve my loan. As a sales professional on a commission-based income, this wasn't easy. A committed track record as a married couple didn't matter now I was a single mum on my own.

This was a time I learnt the importance of having a manager who has your back.

Understanding what I was going through, he went in to bat for me with the leadership team, who approved an arrangement based on goodwill earned. There were no words for the flood of relief and gratitude I felt that day. It was a gesture I will never forget. Particularly for those who made it happen. They didn't have to. They chose to.

The next hurdle was the bank. I tackled it the same way I tackled every customer, not taking no for an answer. There had to be a way. One, then

Peta Sitcheff

two knocked me back. By the time the third application was made, my hopes were fading, but my determination was not. The day they phoned to reject my application almost broke me. It was two weeks before Christmas on an afternoon I had promised to take my six year old goddaughter to get her ears pierced (much to the relief of her squeamish mother!) On the way to pick her up at the school gate, the bank phoned. I inhaled as deeply as I could, the hairs on the back of my neck standing on end as I tried to digest the dismal news and supress my frustration. The emotionless voice on the other end of the phone confirmed that for the third time my application, my only means for creating a homely nest of my own, had been rejected. Sensing danger, my whole body was burning with high alert. I felt frozen, like the prey in the reticle of a hunter's view.

> I don't want to move to a new house. I can't do that to Lewis. He needs the familiar walls of his bedroom, his favourite place – his bath, the scribbles he has made on the walls, the old vomit marks on the carpet I can't remove. He has been through enough.
>
> I can't disappoint him. I can't.

With the news from the mortgage broker freshly ringing in my ears, I felt like my brain was floating above my body.

> This can't be happening.

The school bell rang and I watched my gorgeous goddaughter come running out, smile ear to ear and white blonde hair in pig tails bobbing away. She threw her arms around me, excited for her big day. Burying my dread, I started the car. I had to shift gears.

We walked into the local chemist, where the over manicured beautician, led us through the shelves of cheap fragrances to a tall stool in the corner of the store. Within minutes she aimed her gun through Miss 6's fleshy ear lobe and shot a hole through the centre. Not knowing what she didn't know, the

My Beautiful Mess

first ear was easy. Remembering this painful, burning sensation myself, I took a look at her red-hot ear and waited for the reaction. 1...2...3 seconds then, tears. With the fear of god in her, she now didn't want to second ear pierced. "For the love of god, your mother will kill me!" I thought.

"We've got this kiddo," I assured her. "How about we get a bag of jellybeans after this?"

She nodded. I had a quiet word to the beautician.

"Big breath, look in my eyes chicken," I said, offering cold comfort for what was about to happen next. Her big blue eyes brimmed with tears and gazed at me bravely. I took her hand.

"1...." I winked at the beautician.

"2...." BANG!

Startled by the surprise, Miss 6 jolted upright, her eyes as wide as dinner plates. It was over. Realising what had just happened, tears of fear were replaced by tears of relief and her infectious nervous giggle. A smile started to emerge and fortunately, no anger, for the little trick I had played. She skipped out of there, blue jewels sparkling in her ears, sucking on a pink "chemist" jelly bean. Goddaughter ear piercing done. Tick.

If the afternoon was an emotional rollercoaster, what happened next was the gradual climb of the cart, before its nose peaked over the top, and tipped into a roaring steep descent that led into a spiralling corkscrew. Gravitational force pinning you back to your cheap vinyl covered seat.

As we ventured up the High St to buy a Christmas gift for Miss 6's Mum, I started to feel off. Adjusting the rear-view mirror with my left arm so I could see Miss 6 nattering in the back seat, it suddenly turned cold. It was like the blood in my arm became immediately chilled. Then my lips started tingling.

Peta Sitcheff

Ok, I'm not sure about this. Please no. My father had a heart attack at the age of 36... am I having a heart attack? Crap think fast Peta! The GP. If I can get back to Albert Park I'll be okay.

I swung the car into a U-turn across the busy road. As it turned out, I didn't have time to get very far at all. My heart started racing like a ticking time bomb in its final seconds. I couldn't draw breath and was forced into rapid short gasps that didn't fill my lungs. I felt clammy, sweat beads gathering on my upper lip as I grabbed the phone and rang Troy, godfather of Miss 6.

"Something is wrong, I have Miss 6 in the car, I'm on the corner of High Street and The Avenue. I'm ringing an ambulance," I rushed. Then I hung up. I can only imagine how he would have felt in that moment.

I was less worried about me and more for Miss 6 who would be in the car on her own if I passed out.

I rang 000, told them what had happened and as soon as they had the information they needed and assured me they were minutes away, they asked for the phone to be passed to Miss 6. Very shortly, I could hear the siren in the distance becoming louder. The 000 operator chatted away to Miss 6, who had one concerned eye on me, as I was trying to regulate my breathing. I'll never forget how brave she was that day.

The ambos were amazing. An ECG and a blanket for me as a massive rush of adrenalin left me in a violent shaking shiver, and an oversized raspberry slurpee for Miss 6 (that they had bought before my call). On top of the ear piercing she couldn't wait to get to school the next day to tell the class about the excitement that afternoon! It was recommended I head to the local hospital for assessment. With friends now at the scene, Troy came with me to the hospital where I was cleared of any heart issues.

For the first time, anxiety had officially entered my life. The doctors diagnosed

My Beautiful Mess

a severe panic attack.

Eventually, with Troy's gracious help, I managed to get my loan approved.

I had a place I could make our home. We wouldn't have to move. If I couldn't give Lewis a Mum and a Dad under the one roof, at least he would have familiar surroundings. For now.

Getting to the top of Mt Everest, proudly pitching my flag and collapsing with relief in the snow would be how I would describe the moment I knew I owned my home. I had survived the ascent, at times literally required oxygen, dug my ice boots in harder and put one foot in front of the other with intense, focused determination until finally, I had made it.

I could put holes in my walls, buy furniture that properly fit spaces and create that homely feeling I craved. It didn't take long to forget about the mortgage as it morphed into the reality that was monthly household expenses. What I never forgot and still haven't, was the struggle to get that loan over the line.

The handsome income my job provided was one I held onto white knuckle tight. I couldn't and wouldn't let it go, occasionally letting myself wonder how I was going to keep this frenetic pace up for the long haul. I quickly pushed the thought out of my mind too scared to answer a question I knew someday, I would have to face.

For now, I didn't feel I had a choice. It was like I felt my life would always be this constant state. There was no thought of change, only maintenance of the status quo. I look back on it now realising how numb I was to any sort of learning or personal growth. I would have been happy living my life in a snow dome forever, keeping everything on the outside, exactly the same.

I knew what I needed at that point in time to feel safe in life. I had my bricks and mortar, I had a bank account that was handsomely fed each month. My wardrobe shone with designer labels and I travelled the world for business and pleasure. My glossy veneer made me feel successful. That was my definition of life success.

What I hadn't allowed for was change within myself.

Inadvertently, I had signed myself up for a sentence I didn't know existed.

On an emotionally flat day, I was chatting away on the phone with The Director. I'd worked the previous two weekends, and in a day dreamy moment while stopped at a red traffic light, I allowed my curiosity to drift into ominous "what's next?" territory.

"It would be nice to have my weekends back, but how do I jump to a different role, that pays half the salary?" I wondered out loud.

"Ahh, you are bound by the golden handcuffs my dear," he laughed as he reminded me of my predicament.

"What do you mean?" I asked.

It was a term I hadn't heard before and as the words sank in, so did the dreaded reality that he was right. So long as my lifestyle, expenses and self-worth depended on it, I was handcuffed to my income and emotionally dependent on the selling roller coaster. Trapped in a vicious cycle that was hard to back away from. I am sure leaders must rub their hands together when they hear of employees buying new homes. Their high income a big, juicy and enticing carrot that would hopefully, see them stick around for a bit longer.

Were these the shackles I had to unlock to set myself free?

Today's Reflection
-

Panic attacks are a feeling I never forget and now having had more than 1 and less than 5, I know exactly how my onset presents. A cold, left arm and tingling numb lips. It usually happens when I am driving (no idea why) and is followed by a sudden racing heart and breathlessness worthy of an athlete having just crossed the line after a 100 m sprint.

With regulated deep breathing, I can now slow the process and catch it before the adrenalin shakes set in. What comes next, is a need to wipe my slate for the day clean, to take the whole lid off the pressure cooker, not just release the valve. "To do's" get thrown out the window, as I know they will all be there tomorrow. Nothing is ever as urgent as you think it is. I spend my day recalibrating. Doing what I need to slow my brain, manage my emotions and move my body.

Exercise really is good for the soul.

Recommended Reading
-

The Happiness Trap
'Stop Struggling, Start Living'
Dr Russ Harris
Published by Exisle Publishing Limited (2007)

Peta Sitcheff

Ego
-

"Shame corrodes the very part of us that believes we are capable of change"
Brené Brown

I knew I needed "something", but I had no idea what that "something" was.

The minute I started to dream about treading a different path, I became racked with guilt.

>Don't be stupid, you can't go anywhere. They can't survive without you.

After some coercing from my sister, I agreed to meet with her life coach.

>What the heck, I suppose it can't hurt.

That is when Shannah entered my life. A trusted soul who would challenge my thinking and give me the permission I couldn't give myself – to contemplate change.

During our first session, I turned up in my work wardrobe, as stiff as a corpse and with a facial expression to match. The only expression I matched with the designer labels, was sadness.

I couldn't remember the last time I felt happy.

As every good coach should, she plonked me front and centre of the conversation, her back strategically against the bustling café wall, with me sitting directly opposite, facing the wall. It was her way of blocking out peripheral distraction and shielding me from curious stares should I burst into tears.

    She's done this before.

After the first few sessions, we both started to realise how much I had to unravel.

Her questions always cut through the weeds and shot straight to the beating heart of whatever issue we were exploring over our espressos. She was always listening, never judging and despite the bustling hive of café activity around us, always making me feel I was the most important person in that room.

Forever the disciplined student, I would always do my "homework". After one particular session, my homework was to look at myself in the mirror. It sounded simple enough.

Initially, I quite simply couldn't. I stood in my cavern like bathroom, surrounded by travertine, hair wrapped in a fluffy towel turban, my skin shiny clean from its recent gritty scrub. As I lifted my gaze to meet that of my reflection, my eyes instantly repelled, randomly darting around the room

Peta Sitcheff

like they were following tiny glitter flecks from an oscillating disco ball. I tried again and again, but anytime I caught the gaze of the blonde stranger before me, I wanted to run for the hills. Anything to avoid the mounting anxiety that came with this unwanted confrontation.

"For fucks sake, get a grip. Let's try to count to ten" I said to myself out loud.

After a few attempts, I'd forced myself to hold for ten, pushing through the nauseating uneasiness rising from my belly, beads of sweat forming on upper lip as I tried to control my racing heart through long, billowy breaths. The reaction was real and visceral. Determined to push through the pain, I forced myself to go further.

"OK, let's try thirty."

I searched everywhere around my face, noticing a new freckle here, stray eyebrow hair there, then finally, I stopped at my eyes.

> How would I describe their colour? Navy, yep no change after 40 years.

Then I started to notice the layers in my navy eyes like the crystals in a kaleidoscope. Flecks of white, my black pupil dilating and shrinking, making me feel like I was swaying back and forth.

After two or three minutes, the distractions abated, and I remember finally settling on my gaze. It was like I was staring at an ex-lover. Someone I once had a bottomless emotional connection with and knew down to their bare bones. Someone who there and then had the capability to see through my façade, to strip back my armour, leaving a vulnerable and quivering woman before them, tears spilling down her cheeks.

It was a replay of that childhood moment when you are being scolded by a parent and do anything to avoid eye contact. As soon as you do, cue the tears.

My Beautiful Mess

Please don't make me keep looking at this person.

I couldn't run from my reflection or accept what she was telling me despite trying my darndest to avoid it for years. I didn't like who I was either and no, my life wasn't working.

Right there is when I should have thanked my reflection and given her the equivalent of a warm embrace. But I didn't. Instead, I threw a metaphorical stone into the mirror, silencing the voice behind it and put my foot down harder on the existence I knew.

Work harder.

This is who you are Peta. You don't have the luxury of choice, too many people rely on you.

I guess I could curtail the lavish online spending on Valentino studded flats I didn't need? Hang on, I deserve it. I work bloody hard.

Besides, it completes the picture everyone expects to see.

Over the years, I had become a maestro artist attempting to create a façade worthy of a place in the Louvre. Attempting, or so I thought, because I naively thought those around me couldn't see through it. I was an impressionist creating the best impression I knew how. Luxury fashion labels were my medium of choice. As my confidence plummeted, I craved material rewards, it was the only way I knew how to feel better about myself.

Impulsive spending motivated the impressionist within me and inflated my shrinking ego balloon. Human mannequin sales professionals, welcomed me into their showroom with open arms, greeting me by name.

Peta Sitcheff

"This would be magnificent on you!" they'd coo. "Let me slip these into the change room," knowing full-well that once they lured me in behind those 8-foot-high curtains, the adrenaline would take over and I wouldn't be able to resist. The reflection staring back at me was the perfect façade, the armour a perfect shade of sky blue.

    This will more than do.

For them, I was a sure thing. For me, I felt immune to consequence. It was a reckless combination.

As I walked to the register for the grand finale of the spree, I'd flippantly sign off the multi- thousand dollar Mastercard docket, knowing the money wasn't in the account to cover the cost.

    You can't keep this up. You didn't need any of that.

    But I have to maintain the Peta everyone expects.

    It's who they think I am.

I'd push the curt tone in my head away as I put the many giant rectangular glossy bags in the back seat of the car. I would make it into the driver's seat just before the inevitable dreaded feeling of shame would kick in. I was secretly embarrassed I couldn't control my impulses but then, like a pre-programmed robot, I'd just turn up the radio to drown out the preaching in my head.

Deep down I knew, like any child caught with their hand in the cookie jar, I was spending well beyond my means and would one day pay the price. There wasn't anyone holding me to account. There was no need to hide my purchases like shameful secrets, under the bed or in the boot of the car. No one was watching over me, or my bank balance. No one, except my conscience that is. As I walked into my bedroom and caught the gaze of my reflection in the mirror, I quickly stuffed the bags into my overpacked

My Beautiful Mess

wardrobe, hiding them from my judgemental eyes.

My impulsive spending dressed my ego and allowed me to create the artwork others could judge. They weren't the only ones judging my superficial reflection - I was too. I was desperate for them to recognise that I was a fake, a forgery and not really as good as they thought. I felt like I was operating like a robot dressed in designer clothes, to the point where I even started describing myself that way at work.

"If you want me to do something differently, I'll have to reprogram myself," I'd say.

"Discipline" sat in my top five strengths and was proudly framed in The Director's office. Every time I looked at that frame, it reinforced my behaviour was unchangeable.

Recommended Reading
-

Ego is the Enemy
"The Fight to Master our Greatest Opponent"
Ryan Holiday
Published by Profile Books Limited (2017)

The Gifts of Imperfection
"Let Go of Who You Think You're Supposed to Be and Embrace Who You Really Are"
Brené Brown
Published by Hazelden Publishing (2010) p. 41.

Peta Sitcheff

The Spine Girl
-

"We should also regularly doubt ourselves, and question what has shaped our own thinking, what unconscious biases we might harbour, and whether we might be wrong. All of us have limited understanding of most things, most especially the lived experiences of other people"

Julia Baird

Always curious and with much trepidation, I thought I'd try to dip my toe into the water to explore change on the softest landing pad I could find. It was time to speak to The Director. He was always in my corner and knew which buttons to push on the robot to bring out my best.

My Beautiful Mess

He read me well, guiding me when I asked and being firm when I deserved a clip. Mostly, he gave me the autonomy and space I needed to spread my wings and run the business I was caretaking as though it was my own. Rarely did I receive any pushback, even when I knew deep down, I was pushing the envelope a little too hard.

Surely, this conversation would be no different. Heck, it should be even more important. It was about me.

Here I was, lost in the professional wilderness with no survival skills and no plan.

"Surely he can help?" I wondered naively. I knew I needed to pick up the phone and talk but had no idea how to entertain the conversation. I guessed I'd do what I always did, just start.

On a sunny afternoon when I had time to spare until my next appointment, I parked my car in a cul-de-sac on Richmond Hill offering beautiful panoramic views of Melbourne. Thinking that at least the stunning outlook might balance out the familiar clench that was getting tighter around my stomach by the minute.

I wasn't sure The Director would take my wobbles seriously, predicting that while he might squirm in his leather Eames chair for a minute or two, like any professional athlete going through a slump, he would be pretty confident he had the persuasive power to talk me back on the track. He always knew what to say to rev me up.

In reality, that call was the first flare I fired. My warning straight to the top that I might be in a pickle and was having trouble finding my oxygen mask.

I remember the conversation as if it were yesterday.

"If I wasn't in sales, what else could I do?" I naively asked, more curious than fearful.

Peta Sitcheff

"What would you like to do?" The Director asked in a tone clearly humoured by my question.

That was the $1 million-dollar question constantly thrown my way and my answer was always the same: I had no idea. The strategy put the onus back on me, but from my perspective, I didn't know what I didn't know. It just made me feel even more lost in an environment that was as familiar as home.

It was what came next that left me feeling like I had had a giant post-it-note slapped on my forehead. The impact left me dazed in disbelief, with stars circling around my blonde head.

"Why would you change? You're the Spine girl," he smirked.

I felt like I'd been hit in the face with a wet sponge.

> Wake up Sitcheff! After 12 years of delivering year after year, that's all you are. The "Spine girl"! It may as well be scribed in big cursive letters along a satin sash worn over my surgical scrubs. How elegant.

I'd always been so proud of my work and the comment felt strangely demeaning. It was as though I was being shoved into a pigeon hole that was wired by other peoples perceptions and that is where I would stay. My wings clipped.

> You've been told. That's where you fit in the eyes of everyone. In the eyes of the company you're another cardboard cut out. You're the Spine girl.

As the words sunk in and before I had a chance to think of a polite response, the next shot was fired.

My Beautiful Mess

"You know you will never earn the sort of money that you do now if you move to another part of the business?"

> That old chestnut. Do all of the leaders in the organisation realise they say the same thing word for word?

It felt like a defensive move straight from a leadership playbook. A chorus of voices attempting persuasion to protect the numbers that pay their bonuses.

I found it ironic that as a sales professional, I was the customer to my leader and in this case, there was no effort to explore where on earth these feelings were coming from. Rather, the choice was to appeal to my ego. To appeal to my materialistic needs by dangling the financial incentive hook. Yep, I was the fish and I had taken the bait. I had done that all along and as predictable as the rising sun, I had again.

It played into my fear perfectly.

> Of course, I need this income. What was I thinking?

But "the Spine girl?" I couldn't dismiss so easily.

As I hung up the phone that afternoon on Richmond Hill, I couldn't shake the feeling of being misunderstood. Like I wasn't being taken seriously.

I started to realise this landing pad might not be as soft as I thought.

> Crash mat maybe?

Peta Sitcheff

Today's Reflection
-

Beneath the façade and superficial nuances within us, we are all complex beings craving to be understood. Our brains energised by our four core needs, a sense of meaning, connecting with others, continual learning and giving back to society. (Murden, Defining You) I've always thought it is up to us to make the effort to learn rather than judge another, galvanising them unfairly in time. Firmly believing that if someone appears perplexing, it is more than likely we just don't understand them well enough yet. That is on us.

Perhaps I am looking at an adult world through the rose-coloured glasses of a child, but I wish leaders in business would better recognise the beating heart of a human behind the printed employee ID on their head count chart. Too often, playbook conclusions are leapt to, without exploring what is actually important to the emotional person in front of them. In all likelihood, they might be surprised when they dig a little deeper and realise the superficial problem, really isn't the problem at all.

It's a gap that can be bridged, so long as we are willing to don a different lens and consider for a moment that our answer might not be the only answer. That there might be merit in challenging our thinking and venturing down the path of curiosity, exploring any doubt until it crystalises into a certainty. It is still an informed decision, just one validated through a process of growth rather than fixed lens of bias. After all, it would be negligent not to consider the risk to the business if you were to do nothing at all.

Recommended Reading
-

Phosphorescence
"On Awe, Wonder and Things that Sustain You When the World Goes Dark"
Julia Baird
Published by HarperCollins Publishers Australia (2020)
p. 154, 264.

You're Not Listening
"What You're Missing and Why it Matters"
Kate Murphy
Published by Penguin Random House UK (2020)

Peta Sitcheff

Outliers
-

"Here's to the crazy ones, the misfits, the rebels, the troublemakers, the round pegs in square holes...the ones who see things differently – they're not fond of rules...You can quote them, disagree with them, glorify or vilify them, but the only thing you can't do is ignore them because they change things...they push the human race forward, and while some might see them as the crazy ones, we see genius, because the ones who think they can change the world, are the ones who do."

Steve Jobs

My treasured clinical team at work were a group of special individuals with huge hearts. All of us bound by the sheer determination only a group of outliers could ever understand.

My Beautiful Mess

For years, the Spine division of the company was the poor cousin of the family. We didn't have the large teams or financial resource that the broader organisation had, artificial knees and hips being the stars of the show. They were market leaders, the flagship teams. If they rose to the occasion, the company shone, and the share price skyrocketed. We were side B of the disc. The "wooden spooners". The team that had to "repolish the turd," I once heard The Director say in a loose moment, so slow was the pace of innovation and archaic our technology.

I reckon we made that turd shine with the volume of business we pumped through.

Known for biting off more than I could chew, "outlier" was a description I'd always unwittingly chased, thriving on the challenge it necessitated. I'll never forget the day I had made a day trip to Sydney for a "Know your Strengths" workshop. It was one of a series of assessments adopted by the company. From those that determined the fate of a potential employee, to others that acted as the connective tissue of the workforce, that is once you had survived the marathon recruitment process and officially made it through the door. Those assessments ran through the veins of the organisation.

"What's your top five?" was a question commonly asked amongst the corridors, the long hallways dressed in polished timber honour boards listing worthy award winners from years gone by.

I was fascinated by the spooky accuracy an algorithm could demonstrate when it spat my strength profile from its highly engineered motherboard. Did it's artificial intelligence really know me better than I knew myself?

As I read my profile, the printing perfectly centred on the manicured page, I couldn't help but feel the humanism had been squeezed out of what should have been a deeply personal journey of self-discovery.

Peta Sitcheff

The words I was reading described the "how" to my behaviour. Descriptions that reflected what I cherished most. They should have been woven into the tapestry of my life, along with the thread of my personal values, but this felt clinical.

Only one person on this earth could truly understand my spiritual compass and that person had a heartbeat and blonde hair, not a log in ID and password.

For the time being, my "top five" strengths were displayed for public view, frozen in a photo frame above The Director's desk.

The very thought of it made me want to smash that frame and throw its labelling connotations in the bin.

On this particular day in the boardroom, there were 20 of us standing in the centre of the room. We were asked the question "You finish your working week and it has been really stressful. What do you prefer; to be on your own? Or, to go and socialise with your friends to let off steam?" It was an interesting exercise. 19 people went to one side of the room, they wanted to socialise. One person went to the other side. That one person was me.

> Oh god, there are 19 pairs of eyes looking at me. Stop staring! I feel like a freak. Like I'm shrinking. What's wrong with you? You don't fit in here.

My heart rate quickening with the unwanted attention from across the room. I felt too big for my body, my clothes no longer large enough to house the voices in my head. My skin started crawling as I became overwhelmed by the sense of wanting to cut myself free of the skinny denim jeans that were strangling my legs. My eyes darted around the room frantically looking to flee from the ensuing episode I found myself in.

Isolation, loneliness, alienation. Three words of the same vein, all with very different meanings. In that moment, I felt an awkward combination of all three. It was no-one's intent to embarrass me, but it was hard to know how those other 19 people perceived me from then on.

I was in a room full of people but felt totally alone.

Recommended Reading
-

Outliers
"The Story of Success"
Malcolm Gladwell
Published by Penguin Books (2009)

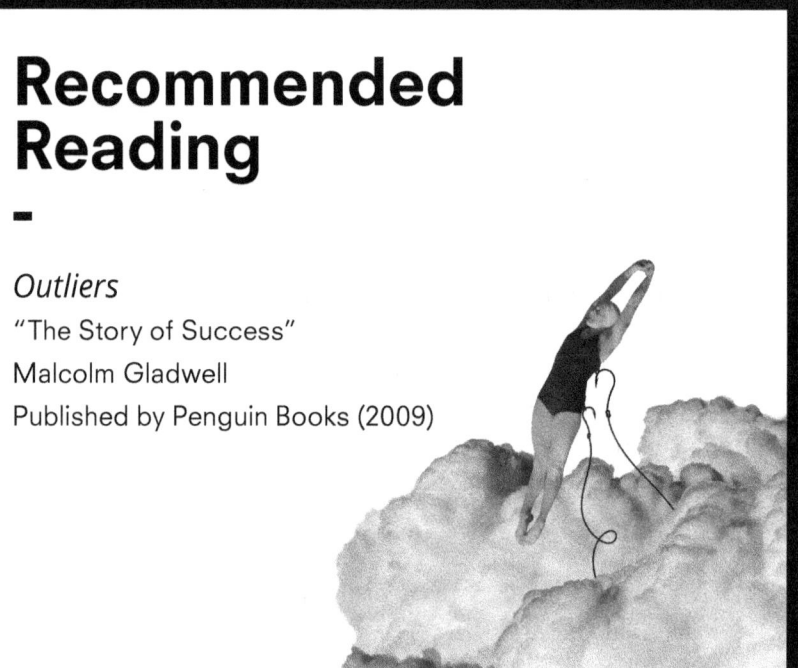

Peta Sitcheff

Niggles
—

"What you think about you bring about. It's so funny, the stuff that I really focused on and was upset, nervous and anxious about was the shit that wasn't working, it didn't work, and it continued to not work until I let it go"

Zoë Foster Blake

It was an unfamiliar sensation that nagged at every step I took, like a foreign mass that had snuck into my body and was invading my cells. First, it was every once in a while, infrequent enough to dismiss. Then it would linger for a few hours like a dull hangover. With time, the episodes would string together for a run of successive days.

I didn't recognise the feeling. It wasn't the usual pressure cooker stress of trying to juggle too many things at the same time. It was more like a dark veil of unhappiness clouding my view and no matter how I tried to look after myself, I couldn't lift those ominous, depressive clouds.

Blemishes were revealing themselves on my confidence each day that I could

My Beautiful Mess

no longer heal with the superficial band aids that had worked in the past. I wasn't just tired, I felt hollow. Young, new, fresh faced colleagues would come bouncing in full of enthusiasm, excited they had finally broken into the medical device industry. Meanwhile, I was struggling to put one foot in front of the other, becoming a hardened, pessimistic stranger to myself.

Who the heck was this person?

In truth, I felt like a square peg jammed in a round hole. I wondered why my usual routine that had served me well for 13 years suddenly, no longer felt right.

As fast as the inconvenient questions appeared, I shoved them out of my brain. I couldn't deal with their invasion right now, even if they were trying their darndest to send me a warning signal that troubling times were looming. I pressed pause on those warning signals, thinking it was familiarity I needed to feel safe.

For a long time, I'd accepted this was the way my life was meant to be. It was as though my script was written.

It wasn't until my oldest friend who had known me for 32 years said to me over the airwaves "Pete, your life has always been so damn hard" that I began to think otherwise.

I never realised that was how I was perceived, nor had I ever contemplated the thought life could be any different. "Isn't it like this for everyone?" I wondered. While I didn't realise it at the time, that passing comment planted a tiny seed of hope that I would later reflect upon, when I was trying to muster the courage to face that fear head on.

For now, freezing myself like a polaroid in a hard existence seemed a much more desirable option than free falling through the unknown. Little would those around me understand the inner turmoil intensifying behind the

Peta Sitcheff

highlight reel. There were a small handful who really knew me and could see the cracks starting to form.

My dear girlfriend's words continued to echo around my head as I kept reminding myself of Mum's words, "Pete, ignore a niggle at your peril."

I like to think of my niggles as the softly spoken voice of my gut. My personal values that give me a timely nudge when I'm not listening. They generally start by speaking to me in a kind whisper, like a polite stranger reminding me that they are in charge. "Something isn't right. You might want to course correct here Pete" they say kindly like a wise old owl, protectively looking over me.

If I continue to shoo them away like an unwanted cat rubbing against my leg, they might give me a poke in the ribs or a shove in the shoulder. If that doesn't get through, the yelling starts, which if I am obstinate enough to ignore, and continue to bury my head in the sand, they take matters into their own hands and send a deeply visceral message.

"If you won't listen to us, we will make you listen Peta" they barked. I always knew I was in trouble when my whole name was used rather than just Pete. As a kid, that was the sign I had pushed Mum or Dad too far. With all of the determination I could muster, I slammed my foot on the accelerator on this life that was no longer serving me well. A gesture my niggles didn't appreciate in the slightest. Fair to say they took the reins and found a way to start relieving the rising pressure within me.

Like a population hit by a deadly contagion overnight, my hair suddenly died. One day it was alive and thriving, the next, dead. It wouldn't have been irrational to think someone had booby-trapped my shampoo with poison. I was blow drying it after a routine wash and suddenly, clumps all over my head started turning a burnt orange. The distinct smell of burnt keratin filled my nostrils as my hairbrush filled with clumps of straw like hair.

My Beautiful Mess

What the fuck? Christ there really is something seriously wrong with me.

I leaned into the mirror for a closer inspection. The hair was frizzled and when I rubbed it between two fingers, it disintegrated into dust. I hadn't done anything differently from my normal blow dry. Weird. Too scared to dry anymore, I padded the rest of my hair gently with a towel and could see where patches of my wet hair had turned to jelly. It was like I had clumps of wet, thin rice noodles all over my head. When it was wet the "noodle hair" had an abnormal amount of stretch until it snapped. It took hours for the moisture to evaporate, but when it did it became immediately delicate, snapping off about an inch from my head in clumps. My poor hairdresser was beside herself. Good bye long hair. Welcome short, rust-stained straw.

The rest of my body wasn't much better. The kilos had started dropping off as my hunger disappeared. I felt like someone had their hand clenched around my stomach and I wore an exhaustion on my face that no amount of good quality concealer could disguise.

Worst of all, was the pain. It was excruciating. Over the course of two years, I'd developed a neuropathic electrical pain that I had no doubt was directly linked to my stress levels. The pain was numb by day and flared at night. My head would finally hit the crisp pillow, the warmth of the thick woolly underlay beneath me. It always made me feel like I was floating on a cloud, a welcome relief after a 12 hour day of standing in an operating room dressed in heavy lead aprons. But rather than feel my muscles relax, my skin was suddenly invaded by the feeling of burning, red hot forks running up my forearms and calves. It was like someone had lit a bonfire within me and was "burning off". The stress from the day just gone, being released through my nerve ends. Vacating them of any tension so they could refill the very next day.

The routine was the same every night. First the burn off, then the smouldering ache. Each of those muscles became engulfed in a drawing pain that no body position, muscle stretch, or amount of rest would relieve. Movement and water were the only things that worked. When my brain needed sleep and my eyelids needed to close, my muscles needed to pace the hallway to stop the agonising chronic pain. 3am Radox baths became a thing. The pain interrupted my sleep, as did the baths, making the next day hard.

Every day was becoming bloody hard. Enthusiasm and inspiration had become replaced with tedium and dread, but still I wouldn't budge. I was like a two-year-old clutching onto their parent's leg not wanting to be separated.

I was desperate to find a way to stay shackled to this life, so I didn't have to face the alternative: Change.

Recommended Reading
-

Untamed
"Stop Pleasing, Start Living"
Glennon Doyle
Published by Penguin Random House UK (2020)

Dying to Be Me
"My Journey from Cancer, to Near Death, to True Healing"
Anita Moorjani
Published by Hay House Australia (2012)

Work Well Being
"Leading Thriving Teams in Rapidly Changing Times"
Mark McCrindle & Ashley Fell
Published by Rockpool Publishing (2020)

Peta Sitcheff

Disconnection
—

"Why do you stay in a prison when the door is so wide open?"

Rumi

Everyone wanted a piece of me. Every day I was being picked at by a committee of circling vultures and all that was left were the scraps and a putrid carcass.

The surgeons needed me in the operating room. My phone rang constantly with spot fires that needed extinguishing. The Director wanted to know the reason behind the declining sales numbers. An unexpected and unfamiliar trend on my usually glowing sales reports.

My Lewis deserved my presence, but more often than not was graced with my mental absence.

Friends phone calls were left unanswered and the envelopes of bills piled up unopened on the kitchen bench.

My Beautiful Mess

I was desperate to be relieved from responsibility. To find my own secret hiding place where no one could reach me, by person or by phone. I wouldn't be interrupted by any ring, ping or alarm, my ears wouldn't be invaded by noise nor my brain violated by distraction.

The pause in life created by long haul flights was always a welcome escape. I could float in the air, totally weightless of duty and experience the overwhelming stillness that came from something I could never achieve at sea level – connecting with myself.

From the moment I changed my voicemail in the lounge letting any caller know I was not going to feel one ounce of guilt for not taking their call, I had signed off. Gone. I'd plonk myself in that reclining airline seat and begin my onboarding ritual. It was sheer bliss. I'd pull on my fluffy woollen socks, set up my paw-paw cream and rose hand cream, my note pad and pencil, don my noise-cancelling headphones and put Meryl on the screen. I had assumed the position for 14 hours of splendid isolation and would soak in every minute of my freedom in the clouds.

No one could get me and if the person sitting next to me tried, the eye mask, ear phones and beanie would go on. It was the best "closed for business" sign I could manage.

The returning trip was never quite as exhilarating. Anticipation for what would be waiting at the other end when I turned my mobile phone back on, building with each hour. I'd turn my phone on once we landed and it would start pinging incessantly. Each ping adding another item on to my "to do" list.

I remember when I used to love that ping. Wish for it even. Now it poked at my nerves. The anticipation enough to keep me on a continuous nervy edge, resentment building for the palm sized screen that had come to dictate my life. For 13 years I had willed it's call, now I craved its silence, or so I thought.

It became a love hate relationship.

Peta Sitcheff

Why isn't the phone ringing? You're clearly losing your touch. You won't have enough to pay for things. You won't be able to keep this life up.

Obsessively, I'd keep checking that touch screen to make sure it still had a pulse.

Your run is over Peta. Your customers are choosing your competitors over you now. Your time is up. You aren't good at this anymore. No one wants you.

No one.

Then, from the deafening silence, my iPhone would musically ping.

A booking! OK I've got this.

Just like that, the valve of the internal pressure cooker was opened. The anxious thoughts would be frantically released like a bullet escaping its chamber. The crowded space replaced by an overwhelming sense of relief. Although I didn't entirely believe it.

Recommended Reading
-

The Obstacle is the Way
"The Ancient Art of Turning Adversity to Advantage"
Ryan Holiday
Published by Profile Books Ltd (2015)

Digital Minimalism
"On Living Better with Less Technology"
Cal Newport
Published by Penguin Random House (2019)

Deep Work
Cal Newport
Published by Hachette Book Group (2016)

Peta Sitcheff

Tipping Point
–

"Now is the time to understand more, so that we may fear less"
Marie Curie

I had no idea what I wanted. All I did know, was I no longer wanted this.

After years of accepting this was my life, fear of an unknown future suddenly felt less scary than the reality of staying where I was.

Finally, I understood what the niggle had been trying to tell me.

> I don't have to be unhappy, I have been choosing to be unhappy. I don't need the large income, I have chosen the lifestyle that needed the income. I'm not defined by my strengths, I have just allowed myself to be defined by my strengths. I wasn't a label, I was a person. I have a choice. Everyone has a choice and I do too.

As the amplitude of my decision sank into my bones, I could feel the weight

My Beautiful Mess

of burden lifting from my shoulders.

> I'm ready to sign off this chapter. I'm not sure what's next but I'll work it out. I always do. There's no reason that strategy should fail me now.

It was shortly after this light bulb revelation that my late Nan had a heart attack back in my hometown, Brisbane. Beautiful Nan was almost 100 years old at the time. She was the matriarch of our family, her presence and voice always grounding me to home, sending me back to my 8 year old self. Nan was a regular presence in my childhood. Her and Pop's weekly Friday visits brought rituals into the household, forever ingrained in my brain. The "money fairy" who would leave a $2 coin on my pillow, the aromas from her home cooked, cheesy smoked cod rice. The blandness of her green vegetables, boiled within an inch of their lives, their chlorophyll and vitamin D washed down the sink with the discarded water.

Nan had a way with people. She 'got' me. From the minute I walked through the door after school, she could tell from the look on my face what mood I would be in. She knew exactly when to get the "punching bag" out, relieving my pent-up frustrations into a pillow that still smelt of starch from its freshly pressed linen case. Fragile with the news of her cardiac turn, I felt drawn to be with her and Mum.

Snapping into work mode, I sorted the household, paused work, booked a flight and took off to the airport all within an hour. I was halfway there when I suddenly realised I had left my work phone on the cold concrete kitchen bench at home, personal phone warmly tucked away in my upper jacket pocket, close to my heart.

After 13 years, that phone was like a prosthetic extension of my arm. It was there for everyone else's convenience except for mine. That moment, in the back seat of a dirty taxi, I decided to amputate.

Peta Sitcheff

For the first time, it would be there for my convenience not everyone else's and as irresponsible as it should have felt, it didn't. I left it on the kitchen bench, happily forwarded the message and for the first time in years, very easily forgot all about that part of my life while I was away. Best of all, I didn't feel bad about it or like I was letting anyone down.
All of a sudden, I could feel again.

As always, seeing Nan was grounding, every minute filling my cup a little more. In her true stoic fashion, it became pretty clear after a few days she was on the mend and would live to see another day. I will always treasure those hours alone we had in her hospital room. She looked small and frail swallowed by the large white hospital pillows. Her mind, anything but. Like always, she looked at me with her piercing blue eyes, cut through the crap and hit me between the eyes with her wisdom.

"Pete, enough."

>Nan's right. I'm done. I'm not living a life. I'm living an unhealthy existence that's making me miserable and slowly tearing me apart.

Arriving back home in Melbourne, it was time to face work. And I tried to, I really did. But when I got into the car the very next day I physically couldn't do it. My hands shook violently on the steering wheel, the tears poured down my face. It was as though Nan was controlling my body and wouldn't let me ignore her words. I would resign by the end of the week, but it wouldn't go according to plan.

There was only one person I could deliver this news to, The Director. The person whose opinion mattered most. His jovial voice on the phone, making me draw a deeper breath to deliver what I knew would be an unexpected surprise.

"I was going to call you this afternoon" he said with enthusiasm.

"Really?"

My Beautiful Mess

"I've got some great news, you know your application for Operation Smile? "

Oh no, not now.

My courage bubble deflated as I could feel my body sink into the chair. Each year, the global organization selected eight employees worldwide to be a part of a team mission with Operation Smile to a third world country. The attendees were part of a clinical team, there for a short time to operate on children with cleft palate defects. It was such meaningful and important work and the thought of being a part of it had lit a fire in my belly I hadn't felt in years. I had been so preoccupied with my own internal struggle, I'd completely forgotten about the application I'd submitted months prior.

"You've been selected" he said proudly.

"You're joking?" I replied in disbelief. "I was ringing you to hand in my resignation"

We both sat there in disbelief for a few moments wondering what the heck was going on in the airwaves between us. The moments we were both expecting, absent and instead replaced with unexpected swirling emotions that just made no sense there and then. True to form, The Director recovered well, buying us both some much needed thinking time.

"Look Peta I don't think you want to make any rash decisions. I know it's been hard on you," he said smoothly.

I couldn't speak and simply nodded silently.

"And I'd hate to see you turn down such an incredible opportunity. Will you at least sleep on it?"

"I need a break. I just can't keep working like this," I said.

Peta Sitcheff

Inside I was in turmoil.

> But I can't think anymore! I've done so much thinking in the past weeks and months. I need to be free.

Not wanting me to leave, nor renege on the Operation Smile offer, we landed in a place that saw me take the rest of the year off, giving me the space I needed, to mentally and emotionally breathe.

Those subsequent months were exhilarating to start. I knew I had left my old job behind, the endless never ending work cycle of being on call around the clock. The responsibility. The phone calls. Managing the surgeons moods. I was done. I finally had my time back. The future was semi-unknown but for now, I was happy with that. I hadn't quite left the nest. The environment would still be familiar, I just didn't know what role I would play in it. It was like I had unlocked the shackles, but they were still around my ankles reminding me of their discrete presence.

As the end of the year drew nearer, the grip of those shackles tightened. Every time I had to jump onto a phone brief regarding Operation Smile, I was given a firm tug.

This wasn't how I managed this experience being. I wanted to be proud of the place I had earned. Instead, the old feeling of insecurity bubbled up to the surface.

> What does the rest of the company think? I'm not at work. Who mysteriously takes three months of spontaneous leave. I'm a fraud. A failure. I can't even manage to do something as simple as quit a job.

I knew my heart had moved on from the company that had been my family for 13 years.

My Beautiful Mess

Breaking the news had loosened the shackles. But I wouldn't be free until I let the opportunity go. I couldn't do it under these conditions, it wasn't right. Hopefully, they would fill the place with someone who had the enthusiasm the opportunity deserved.

Recommended Reading
-

The Untethered Soul "The Journey Beyond Yourself"
Michael A. Singer
Co-published by New Harbinger Publications & Noetic Books (2007)

When to Jump
"If the Job you have isn't the Life You Want"
Published by Henry Holt & Company (2018)

Self-Fidelity
Cassandra Goodman
Published by Cassandra Goodman (2020)

Peta Sitcheff

The Gap
-

"The only way an idea can manifest in our world is through collaboration with a human partner. It is only through a human's efforts that an idea can be escorted out into the ether and into the realm of the actual."

Elizabeth Gilbert

Rather than my already frail confidence sailing through career transition like a yacht skimming through a gentle breeze, I had exposed it to natures fiercest elements – shame and fear. Together, they tossed it around like an inflatable toy through powerful rapids, hurtling towards the edge of a metaphorical cliff.

As the realisation set in that I had bookended a chapter that was more than a quarter of my life, I expected to feel relief. I had shed the voluminous cloak laden with responsibility along with the boxed contents of my car boot at the company warehouse. In true Thelma and Louise style, I thought I was driving off the afternoon I left the company, into the Melbourne sunset exhilarated by a sense of freedom.

My Beautiful Mess

What I really needed, was an oxygen mask and demonstration of the emergency brace position.

Instead of the Hollywood fairy tale, I found myself floundering in an unexpected squally sea of paranoid emotion. The familiar personal floatation devices I was used to were no longer being thrown from the mothership and the safety net of reassurance my work family used to provide, was gone.

My network access denied. I was on my own. I was officially a corporate orphan.

The thunderous thought storms I was trying to get away from had followed me like a second shadow.

> Of course they will all be talking about you. You weren't good enough for them. They didn't try to make you stay. They don't want you. You'll never be good at anything ever again.

The taunting was relentless, constantly implanting stories in my head. To make matters worse, the materialistic pleasures I had relied upon to make me feel good about myself, had gone. Poof. With that final pay cheque date behind me and a credit card already full, I had no idea how I was going to feed the appetite of my hungry ego. I needed for it to feel satisfied for me to feel worth something.

I remember reading *The Reality Slap* by Dr Russ Harris and feeling as though I was living it. His description of the "reality gap" perfectly describing the ravine I was confronted with after being given my rude awakening or "the slap". In my words, a swift kick up the patootie. I had slapped myself hard across the face with this massive life change and was now confronted by the reality of not knowing where I was headed. My elusive destination had created a gap with no end and without that bookend, there was no way to bridge the distance. I was walking on a frayed rope bridge over a raging, white capped, river filled ravine with poor visibility. The mental fog was too dense.

Peta Sitcheff

With each tenuous step; fear, anger, sadness, confusion, loneliness, regret, guilt, resentment, frustration swirled violently beneath me. Treacherous emotionally charged waters that would take their turn sucking me in and spitting me back out.

I felt like I was at the mercy of a force much greater than me. One that was tossing me around like a toy, having fun at my expense. I'd wake up in the morning, not sure what version of myself I would get that day. The sad, the angry, the lonely or the confused. Maybe a smorgasbord of the three would be offered and I'd spend the day changing costumes.

I imagined myself as a tiny being, wandering aimlessly through a streetscape that looked the same but felt vastly different. The view from my bedroom window still showed the coloured city lights after the sun went down, the jacaranda tree on the front pavement still flowered in November, everything was in its rightful place, except me. I couldn't work out where I fit in.

I was swamped with vacant days and hours filled of nothing. The weeks I had Lewis were a blessing. "Mum time" offered structure to my day and became my reason for emerging from beneath the puffy bed covers that kept me safe during the weeks on my own. Our morning walks to school were the best. Lewis would chat away about whatever was in his mind and I would listen, marvelled by how much he knew, saddened by what I had missed, grateful for every second I was clawing back.

I'd drop him off at the gate knowing I'd miss him for the next six hours and would instantly start looking forward to being back in that exact place for the end of day bell. I filled the days pounding the pavement of the local streets, taking haven in my favourite coffee shop. There would be Tuesdays when my Yankees cap would be on, brim down, gaze to the floor. I needed to shut out the world. Then there would be Tuesdays when I was; hat off, eyes up and smile on. I was open for business those days, welcoming a chat and staying for hours. I didn't have anywhere to be, not until that bell rang.

My Beautiful Mess

It was a place that seeded the type of cherished friendships with beautiful, wise souls who would see me on my Yankees cap days, come over and flick up the brim. A gesture that screamed "There will be no shutting the world out today madam. I'll sit here, even if you don't say a word."

I needed friends who knew me better than I knew myself. With my friendships holding me upright, I had to keep believing the fog would clear and the gap would close. That there would be an "other side" that would welcome me with open arms and provide the homely comfort I craved. It couldn't be any opportunity, it had to be something that would make me feel alive again.

As for the voices, well they were fickle. I expected them to be permanently glued to my shoulder during so much uncertainty, but instead all was eerily quiet. I had been so preoccupied by the surface emotions of grief to notice their absence, but there was no denying it was quieter than usual. And it was unsettling.

I longed for what I knew and found it hard to resist being drawn back to a happy place of certainty, the presence of my old customers. In a moment of weakness, I gave in.

Like a delighted child discovering an old photo album of sepia toned family memories, I found myself sitting on my carpeted study floor, sorting through a cupboard of old work paraphernalia. Photos, glass awards, wooden plaques, random screw samples, bold logo lanyards, hand written notes from leaders, an old palm pilot, 13 years of history in a wooden box.

Strangely, they felt lifeless. Items with no emotion, devoid of meaning.

Then I remembered the messages. Messages from colleagues and customers that I had shelved unopened in my inbox. I figured one day I'd be ready to read them.

I sprung to my feet to grab my phone, taking a deep breath as I unlocked the

Peta Sitcheff

screen and clicked onto the until now, dormant folder. I opened them one by one, realising the generic messages I expected were anything but words predetermined by Google. Many of them were deeply personal, expressing sentiments of gratitude for situations that left my memory long ago. Times where I had cared enough to listen on a crappy day or when I had stepped in by way of support, to level out the playing field.

Each sentence was formed by deeply considered words, describing lessons I had unknowingly taught along the way. To me, I was working the only way I knew how.

Tears stung my eyes, as I stepped outside the grieving process for that single moment and allowed myself to grab the emotional lifeline thrown by the memories.

The comments were like a comforting hug, the warmth both overwhelming and humbling. Even the masked surgeon who had said, "Don't be stupid" and hung up on me when I broke the news over the phone, made me smile with his follow up voicemail. He was so predictable and a big softie under the bravado.

Amidst the white-water of my resignation aftermath, it was this post-script that gave my professional chapter in the operating room meaning. Value I never truly realised or appreciated until after I had hung up my theatre clogs.

I found it ironic, that I had to close that chapter in my life to fully realise that impact.

Sifting through the sentiments of gratitude, not a word was uttered about rewards or achievements or anything tangible I could touch. Each described the difference I made as a person. I quickly began to realise, that my true legacy wasn't the wealth I created. In fact, it wasn't material at all. It was simply, me. What I represented, not the company, nor the product.

My Beautiful Mess

For years the value of my professional pride was wrapped up in feel good "flashes in the pan." Tangible achievements and rewards gifted when I hit my sales quota. Outside of the company bubble, none of it mattered. It was of $0 value to my professional reputation.

My legacy stemmed from my values, not my valuables.

Understanding my influence became an unexpected and deeply humbling honour. The experience offering a fresh realisation and newfound sense of responsibility.

The realisation that eyes were watching, and ears were listening, to me. That people believed in what I stood for and were aspired to take a leaf out of my book. I suddenly realised the privilege of the position. One earned through the lessons taught by my missteps and the decision I made to learn from those teachings and better myself as a result. None of it was presented on a silver platter under a cloche.

It all came about through constant course correction, bloody hard work and uncompromising values.

Sorting through the letters, I could feel the start of curiosity rumbling inside of me. The wheels beginning to turn.

> What is possible? What can I do with this information? Uh oh. Something's brewing.

The niggle was back. Not in an unsettling way like the seismic tremor that pushed me down the slope towards burn out. This felt magical. A systemic spark of overenthusiastic inspiration that needed my undivided attention to grow. I could hear Elizabeth Gilbert's words describing ideas as an energetic life-form, ringing in my ears.

I felt instantly compelled to grab this idea with both hands and never let it

Peta Sitcheff

go. I wanted to squeeze every bit of inspiration I could from its veins and relinquish my mind to its energy. Whatever this idea was telling me, it was speaking to my soul.

For the first time in years, I felt truly alive. It was as though I had taken a therapeutic pill that had induced a creative high and taken over not only my body, but my mind, my soul and my emotions. I had so much I wanted to say and so much I wanted to give. I had no idea what my end game would be, all I knew was I couldn't get the ideas out of me fast enough.

That Monday morning after school drop off, in two hours, I redefined my career on my European laundry wall through a frenzied attack of fluorescent coloured post it notes. There I stood, dancing on my own, slapping the wall with bite sized pieces of sticky paper to the tunes of Van Halen. The pressure of the slap proportional to the level of emotion the memory stirred.

It was an unintentional, self-induced dose of psychological therapy, but it wasn't over when the post-its ran out. Then, I hit the sketch books. Grouping the notes into themes, I started to write.

> What made these moments memorable? Why hadn't I forgotten them? How did they make me feel? What was my lesson? Where was the wisdom? What advice would I give my younger self if I were started out again?

The answers started flooding in like a giant oceanic swell, the words literally pouring out of me onto the page. I had so much I wanted to say and while I was saying it to my empty sheet of white paper, I was still feeling connected to the life I was grieving.

It filled a void.

Recommended Reading
-

Legacy
"15 Lessons in Leadership"
James Kerr
Published by Hachette UK (2013)

Incentivology
"The forces that explain tremendous success and spectacular failure"
Jason Murphy
Published by Hardie Grant Books (2019)

The Reality Slap
"How to Find Fulfillment When Life Hurts"
Dr Russ Harris
Published by Exisle Publishing Limited (2011)
p. 2, 11, 44.

Big Magic
"Creative Living Beyond Fear"
Elizabeth Gilbert
Published by Bloomsbury (2016)

Peta Sitcheff

False Start
—

"The last of human freedoms –
the ability to choose one's attitude
in a given set of circumstances"

Viktor E. Frankl

As the words dried up, I felt like I was drifting. Floating in a bubble where the voices couldn't reach me. I guarded my freshly written memories with my life, feeling an umbilical sense of connection with their meaning. Strangely, they made me feel safe. As though they had very delicately started to knit together my emotional wounds. My next predicament was what to do with them, if anything.

Relieved to find myself in calm waters, I was happy to meander through time for a while in the hope opportunity would serendipitously materialize.

My Beautiful Mess

I wasn't in a hurry and it was about all I could manage. It was OK to not jump into the first opportunity that presented, so I kept telling myself. Secretly praying the bubble wouldn't burst.

Eventually, a clue did materialize as I was introduced to a coach who ran her own coaching school and suggested I come along to the first session to see if it interested me. I knew I needed to cultivate a new sense of purpose in my life and that would only come about through new experiences. So off I went.

I walked into a bohemian inspired, warmly lit room. My nostrils were hit with the musky smell of incense. Brightly coloured textiles and well-loved furniture screaming with character, were scattered haphazardly around the perimeter of the room, beckoning my seat. The cosiness instantly put my "first day at school" jitters to ease. We were all there to learn. To build the skills of intense focus and artful communication that would help others through their own life challenges. Or so we thought.

Pairing up, we began practicing on each other. Our real stories coming to the fray, as our "coach" delved deeper through our layers to find what was at the heart of obstructing our ability to move forwards. Between strangers, emotions rose to the surface and streamed from our eyes as vulnerable wounds were exposed.

Every corner of that room was full of powerful, deeply personal healing journeys. The intimacy palpable as we vowed to never share what wasn't ours to share. We thought we were there to learn how to heal others.

The true power in the day, was being introduced to the process of healing ourselves.

Driving home that Friday afternoon, I felt like I was floating. It was as though stagnant, trapped thoughts, had finally started flowing. Even if it was only a trickle, it was movement and it was euphoric. Slowly, the wheels were turning and the vision for my coaching business came to life. My vision was yellow.

Peta Sitcheff

Exploding yellow roses, glowing in the warm sun of a Barossa valley garden became my inspiration, after a fleeting escape on a November weekend. It was a mass of happiness in some stranger's front yard. The sight instantly grounding me to earth and making me smile. Nothing about it was perfectly manicured, it was literally a messy sea of yellow roses that by the thickness of the trunks, looked like they had been allowed to run wild for longer than I was old. I worked like a trojan to pull the business together on the smell of an oily rag.

With enormous trepidation, I launched my website. The "live" date feeling akin to running up the main street of Melbourne CBD naked. A liberating, petrifying and humbling milestone. People phoned just to ask, "how can I help you?" and they did. Clients started to trickle in. I remember my first client session, I was literally on the phone to my own coach 30 minutes prior for a pep talk. I was stone cold petrified. Here I was, about to step off another cliff.

The session flowed beautifully. "Let the client lead you Peta," I kept saying to myself over and over. I walked away, my brain dancing.

I was up and running. I loved the work. I had a brand. I was yellow. My insides should have been glowing with happiness. Instead, I felt empty.

I had been so distracted setting up the business that I hadn't noticed that the fog had lifted in parts. I had fooled myself into thinking the gap was closing. Instead it was ajar and widening again. I was back on the rickety bridge dangling over the ravine.

This time when I looked into the ravine, the presence of the voices was revealed. She had been there all along. Sitting back lounging on a rock, her long legs elegantly crossed, she looked almost statuesque, like she was posing for a cover of Vogue. All this time, she was silently watching, a wry smile on her face. She was waiting to strike, but the timing wasn't quite right.

My Beautiful Mess

She needed to know the spot light would be firmly on her, she'd need to wait for the superficial reactivity of my grief to subside, to reveal the full force of her powerful undercurrent. She had the upper hand over stress, choosing not to mingle with the day to day emotional commoners. She would be patient and wait to make her grandest entrance.

Remember me?

I could feel the undercurrent of grief and anxiety getting stronger and felt myself having to dig my heels into the sand further to not get swept off my feet.

Recommended Reading
-

Man's Search for Meaning
"The classic tribute to hope from the Holocaust"
Viktor E. Frankl
Published by Random House Publishing Group
(2004 recent)

Anxiety
"Expert advice from a neurotic shrink who's lived with it all his life"
Dr Mark Cross
Published by HarperCollins Publishers (2020)

Peta Sitcheff

Back to Bite
-

"If you could kick the person in the pants responsible for most of your trouble, you wouldn't sit for a month."

Theodore Roosevelt

It wasn't enough. I wasn't earning enough money and the stress it created, was preoccupying my every waking moment. My brain felt paralysed to progress. The creative dreams that had run wild only months ago, were now stifled by stress and muted by imminent danger.

While the designer clothes hung silently in my wardrobe, the bills in long white envelopes kept piling in. Now, with flashes of red through their rectangular windows I couldn't ignore.

My Beautiful Mess

I had been treading water for months, trying to keep afloat by plugging holes and buying time as a temporary fix, but the responsibilities didn't stop. They weren't tolerant of the pace it was taking to build my business. To find that magic balance between the coaching work I loved, a strong sense of purpose and the dollars and sense I needed to run my life.

If only time could slow down.

I knew full well it wouldn't. The world was hurtling past at a frenetic pace. I could jump back into a full-time job to permanently plug the holes of my sinking ship, but that would admit failure. Besides, I didn't have the physical or mental strength to contemplate the idea for more than a few minutes.

It wasn't an option, I just couldn't.

Every time I stepped out my front door, I'd don my mask of pretence. The brave smiling veneer that would show the world, I had this. Even if on the inside, I was crumbling. The only person I was fooling it turned out, was myself.

I had no safety net. My time was running out and I was sinking.

> This won't work. Everyone is watching. Everyone thinks you're an amateur. Who are you to think you can do this? They're all laughing at you. You're not free at all – look at the mess you're creating. How are you going to survive like this? You silly, silly girl, get your head out of the clouds. I can't take my eyes off you for even a minute.
>
> You aren't even responsible enough to manage your money. You've thrown it all away and now look at you? You're stuck in a carpark unable to get out.
>
> Pathetic.

Peta Sitcheff

I felt my legs give way and the bile rise to my throat as my entire body caved under her spell. I looked up. There she was cowering over me as I lay shattered on the cold concrete floor of the carpark.

Recommended Reading
-

Burnout
"Solve Your Stress Cycle"
Emily & Amelia Nagoski
Published by Penguin Random House UK (2020)

My Beautiful Mess

Peta Sitcheff

Nice to Meet You
—

"Nothing in life is to be feared, it is to only be understood. Now is the time to understand more, so that we may fear less."

Marie Curie

"You aren't going anywhere under my watch," were the words of my new psychologist Jo.

"It's time you learnt to sit in it".

    Sit in the grey, dirty dishwashing water and wait for my shit to turn to sugar. Yeah, right.

Jo's words that chronic and acute bouts of anxiety had been with me my

My Beautiful Mess

entire life echoed in my ears. We only have the experience of discovering something for the first time once. This was like discovering I had a conjoined twin that had been attached to my brain my entire life and I had no bloody idea.

    I thought I was burnt out. Physically worn out and mentally spent.

    Now you are telling me there is more?

I sat, bewildered while listening to the rationale for my diagnosis. I wasn't perplexed by the mental illness itself. I was astounded by the feeling that someone I had never met before, seemed to know me better than I knew myself. Like she was reciting the "Peta Sitcheff" instruction manual of my behaviours and how they fit together with an Allen key.

The desperate need for self-isolation, my disciplined robotic existence, my obsession for perfect sleeping conditions, my rigidity to stick with "the known"– I thought it was my DNA. If people thought I was difficult they should have spared a thought for me - I had to live with myself 24/7!

I thought I had no choice. Now, I was hearing it wasn't, and I did.

I had unwittingly designed my life to avoid the menace of debilitating anxious symptoms. The more control I had, the more rigid the structure, the stiffer and more predictable my sponge would become. Ironically, there was always warm comfort in the cold, inflexible stiffness.

This existence had controlled the thought storms that crippled my brain and was the only way I knew how to live. It rudely robbed me of desperately needed sleep. It caused many last minute, disruptive decisions as I would fear burdening others if I needed help, the angst mounting in the days leading up to the decision in the hope I wouldn't need to ask anyone for help at all. The teeth grinding and clenched jaw, my intolerance for people for no apparent reason. The random agitation triggered by raw noises and the messy layered

Peta Sitcheff

sounds that flicked the switch to a bad day, instantly.

> My whole life has been created to avoid anxiety, but all I have done is bred it.

I sat there digesting this information in disbelief.

Sitting on Jo's couch, scenarios from over the years flashed before my eyes like an episode of "This Is Your Life." I became overcome with emotion and flooded with an intense, visceral feeling of warm relief, like the warm oil of an Indian Shirodhara treatment hitting my third eye and trickling down the back of my skull.

If Jo's red leather couch could talk, I am sure there would be a Hollywood blockbuster in the stories it could tell. In her room, as I watched the passing minute hand on the wall clock, I felt the cuddle of that couch, my tense body beginning to relax, muscle by muscle, my furrowed brow smoothing for the first time in months. I think my eyes had even begun to smile.

> This isn't me. This life where I constantly feel like I am pushing shit up hill, that takes gallants of effort, that feels hard and rigid, no longer has to be. Maybe I could be happy?

I was suddenly being offered a permission slip. On it, the teacher had written "you are to stop this existence" and offered hope that I was capable of a different, warmer and happier life, but there was a caveat. First, I had to commit to doing something I had never done before. I had to get to know this conjoined stranger that had been in the driver's seat of my life for 40 years and educate it on the rule changes ahead.

I had to get to know her.

She was going to have to move into the passenger seat as a new driver was about to grip the steering wheel. That driver was me.

My Beautiful Mess

"You will get through this," Jo said.

"But for now, it is going to be unpleasant. I don't want you concocting your escape route. Together we will strip you back to basics and rebuild you from the inside out."

I had only ever been properly reprimanded once in my life. It was a 15 minute lunch time detention in high school, a strict, all girls Grammar school in Brisbane. My punishment was for a cheeky drawing of a caricature of my maths teacher that, well, let's say it exaggerated her most prominent facial feature – her (rather long!) nose.

In that moment with Jo, I felt like that 14-year-old child again. I knew I wasn't being punished, but I was being asked to do something I had never in my life done before – restrain myself and be mentally still.

> How on earth am I going to do this on my own?

I needn't have worried, Jo was all over it. She had enlisted my "Three Wise People", Troy, my sister Tina and my dear Dr Pete. I didn't have to do a thing. They became my trio of keepers, their couches forming my safety net for the turbulent time ahead.

I was sitting in the eye of an emotional storm.

> I'm a failure. What will people think? I'm a no-one. I'm missing out while I'm sitting here doing nothing.

Each were voices of my damaged self-worth desperately looking for answers. The problem, this time, no one was forthcoming. I was fumbling in the darkness for what felt like an eternity. My brain wanted to be busy rather than idol, occupied rather than vacant. I couldn't make the raging storm stop. I couldn't be on my own. Even if I was mute on the couch, I needed to know people were around me, to feed me, tell me when to go to sleep, to give my eyes something else to look at rather than the blank ceiling in the isolation of my own home. There were buckets, no torrents of tears I couldn't turn off as a lifetime of relief poured out of my soul. I've never known anything like it. I wouldn't have thought it was possible for any one person to have that much moisture their body. I must have rung out every single cell, top to tail. It poured over the burning fire within me until nothing, but a burned-out emptiness remained.

The distant bells of acceptance rang faintly somewhere in the distance.

This conjoined twin was here to stay, I couldn't kick her out. The first step was giving her an identity and accepting she would be with me for life. I couldn't avoid her like the plague or distract myself in the hope she would shrink away like the Wicked Witch of the West after she had been flooded by a bucket of water. No, I was not Dorothy.

As ironic as it sounds, the secret sauce was to open the door and welcome her in like a long-lost friend. "Well, if that is the case" I thought to myself, "she is going to need a name."

I named her Irene.

Irene presented herself, bold as brass, wrapped in a deep purple velvet cloak. "I'm here!!" she sang. No, I was not crazy, nor did I have an imaginary friend. When I first started meditation therapy, I had to describe Irene's image. It made it easier to focus on what she was telling me, what I needed to change in that moment, to tame my wobbles.

I found I was less afraid of something I could visualise. She became less of an unknown. Less of a caged lion, waiting to pounce out of the darkness and take the bait that was me and more like familiar old aunt, who drops in to visit every once and a while for a cuppa. Even if it wasn't always convenient.

My Beautiful Mess

I don't know why, it just helped.

It took some time to get used to my new room-mate. Initially it was like we were two territorial peacocks sizing each other up. Around we would walk in a ceremonious circle never taking our eyes off each other.

Mental stillness turned out to be bloody tough.

Just as I thought I was mastering the process, even for a few minutes, Irene would fly through the door and cast an anxious hook. It was like she had dropped a large jagged rock into my perfectly still mill pond. The ripple effect sending a wave right through me, draining the confidence out of my cells, washing me with the prickly emotion of fear, shrivelling my brain into the stiff, rigid sponge I was desperately trying to eradicate. I'd be back to square one.

I wanted to run. I wanted to avoid her, bury the thoughts, shut them out by busying my brain. Anything to make her disappear and be far, far away, but the more I leapt to this path of least resistance, it was like I was pouring fuel on her fire. The thought storms started raging out of control.

I was left with no choice but to tackle her head on, woman to woman.

It was time for a new game plan. If Irene was going to proudly present her silver platter of anxious thoughts, rather than run, I'd sit with them. I'd allow them to occupy my brain space, but not suck the oxygen out of the air, taking my hard-earned, newly grounded thoughts with them.

I was the one with control over that oxygen flow, not Irene. Years devoid of learning had given her the upper hand as I'd deprived my brain of oxygen, leaving it malnourished like an old, calcified sponge on the side of the kitchen sink.

My coaching path had given it an appetiser to a new life.

Peta Sitcheff

"Please give me more" my learning brain kept reminding me, desperate to be flooded, over laden with so much fresh knowledge it would cry for the forgiveness that came with being wrung out. It wanted to feel the waves of information filling its pores, tunnelling from one chamber to the next, looking for ways to connect the dots, decipher their meaning and crack the code.

The thick outer layer, my crust of resilience, was suddenly fiercely protective of the spongy conduit of my reinvigorated learning brain, determined to cut through the grease and deflect the rubbish I needn't pay attention to.

Now it was time to arm my brain with the mental fitness required to outperform its saboteur. Not an easy task for someone whose ability to concentrate had been hijacked by a woman wearing a purple velvet cloak called Irene. If I neglected her for too long, guaranteed she would do her juvenile darndest to regain my attention.

It was time to fill the sponge and drown out Irene.

Recommended Reading
-

The Brain that Changes Itself
"Stories of personal triumph from the frontiers of brain science"
Norman Doidge, MD
Published by Penguin Random House (2010)

The Power of Full Engagement
"Managing energy, not time, is the key to performance, health and happiness"
Jim Loehr & Tony Schwartz
Published by Allen & Unwin (2003)

Defining You
"How to unlock your full potential"
Fiona Murden
Published by Hachette (2018)
p. 135.

Peta Sitcheff

Books
▄

""""A book never bothers. A book doesn't wheedle. No one has asked you to subscribe, sign up, enter your card details, your user name, your password. The battery never dies. The WIFI never runs out. In an age where we are even more targeted and profiled and mined for information, reading a book allows you to be, for so long as the covers hold you, truly quiet and undisturbed" It is the only time when I feel I am escaping the noise of the contemporary world. Not just the actual noise, but the anxious noise in my head."

Pandora Sykes

I wanted to make the impossible possible.

I couldn't have told you the last time I'd read a full book. My ability to focus on anything had long been poor - a fact I had tried hard to mask at work.

One I was duly reminded of every Summer when the Australian Open rolled around. I enjoyed the tennis and while I could will my body into stillness

My Beautiful Mess

on the couch, my brain would rebel like an obstinate toddler. The thought storms that Irene left in her wake trapped me in my own head like a school of live fish netted on a trawlers deck. Violently, their bodies would flap, fighting for freedom, slapping my skull with their tails, the vibrations causing me no end of agitation. I couldn't find my own hand to hold through the stinky, fishy mess. Let alone connect with anyone or anything else.

Outside of the peaceful pleasures beneath the summer oceans frothy surface, I'd yet to work out how to escape my own head on a Saturday afternoon in metropolitan Melbourne. A day within the confines of my car driving aimlessly to nowhere was preferred to sitting at home trapped in my own head for the day. I would drive for hours, 80's memories whistling through the wireless. Rolling into a small random town, I'd search for the local country bakery where I'd eat what we would affectionately call as kids a wobbly yellow snot block (aka vanilla custard slice) at a white plastic table. After no more than 30 minutes, I'd turn around and follow the white highway dashes home, desperately fighting the sedative spell of the afternoon sun. Another day over, another day closer to work on Monday when I would have a purpose again and Irene would sleep. Phew.

I'd often pick up glossy magazines at the service station on the home route. While I fully intended on reading their editorials on "remarkable, inspiring women," deep down, I knew the only attention they would get from me would be a random flick before bed. If they were lucky, perhaps a turned down corner to flag a Chloë bag that caught my attention. My brain would welcome the pictures and reject the words.

Long conversations with friends were shortened by made up excuses, as my mind, not so discreetly, drifted off to random faraway places that had nothing to do with our conversation. My attention was thinking about Monday night's school pick up, rather than focusing on understanding my friend's shitty day at work. The thought of knowing how obvious it must have been when my mind drifted, is now deeply embarrassing. I thank god coaching trained me otherwise. The people around me deserved better.

Peta Sitcheff

I had to prepare myself for the climb. If I was going to tackle this mountainous peak – Mt Inability to Concentrate- I was going to need a training schedule, a mental fitness boot camp if you will.

I was determined to conquer a book.

The question was "which one?"

I used to walk into a book store and wonder, how do you know? How do you know which coloured spine staring at you on a shelf will tickle your fancy, captivate you for hours on end and give cause to shun the rest of your day all because you are desperate to find out "who did it?".

It reminded me of when I was pregnant and walked into Baby Bunting for the first time. I didn't even make ten steps past the front door. As those glass automatic doors parted, I was greeted by a mountain of nappy boxes to my left and a baby buggy display to the right that wouldn't have looked out of place in a luxury car showroom. To escape the paralysis engulfing my baby brain from the overwhelming choice, I turned on my heels and fled as fast as a seven month pregnant woman could.

I had to break this down.

My first literary challenge would have its work cut out. My initial window of opportunity was never ajar for long before Irene would slam it shut in one of her anxious tantrums, hijacking my attention back to her.

Years ago, Shannah had introduced me to Robin Sharma's podcasts on personal mastery. His voice was meditative. Whenever I needed to still my brain, I would plonk on my couch, my noise cancelling headphones keeping the outside world at bay and allow the dulcet tones of Robin's voice to hypnotise my brain. That was where I would start – *The Leader Who Had No Title*. A short fable that was easy to understand. "Surely this can't be that

My Beautiful Mess

hard?" I thought to myself.

I now understand what people mean when they say, "just start". There was no point in procrastinating, I just had to get on with it. I've always been a disciplined student, but time has taught me, it's a strength that can work for me, or be my worst enemy. When it works for me, we waltz. Life is balanced, and it becomes a brilliant tool for pursuit. When it works against me, we box. Its rigidity creating a breeding ground for my anxiety.

The toll, I beat myself up, lose my flexibility in life and my mental well-being is swept away with the tide.

I started climbing "Mt Inability to Concentrate" one page at a time. If my mind would wander I would stop and not beat myself up over it.

> Easy lady, you haven't failed. You're just not quite ready.

I needn't have worried. One page in a sitting, very soon turned to 10, then a chapter. Next thing you know I found myself flying through 50 pages in a sitting, my brain drinking in the information at a rate of knots. I couldn't have sucked it through a straw fast enough. The more I fed it, the more it wanted.

I imagined my brain with a quizzical look on its face that read "What are you feeding me?" "Why have you been depriving me of this?" Embarrassed by my neglect, I kept going. It was the best apology I could offer.

I was floored by the power of connection I was experiencing with each page I turned, it was visceral. I was reading what I had been feeling. Feelings that had kept me trapped within myself for eons. My own complex personality riddles that I thought no one else could ever understand. It was as though a window of my soul had opened, allowing the light of hope to shine in.

Obsessively, I craved facts. Lessons, theories and shared experiences I could relate to that helped me demystify myself.

Peta Sitcheff

I wanted to understand how I had ended up in this mess and to somehow work out how to never let it happen again. There was something in the spiritual connection I was feeling. I couldn't let it go. A magnetic force was pulling me down this path to drink in as much information as I could manage.

I had an opportunity to resuscitate and rearrange my life by learning the hard way - through experience. I wasn't going to stuff it up now.

From *The Leader Who Had No Title* to *The Monk Who Sold His Ferrari*. From Maya Angelou to Brené Brown. I was *Daring Greatly* and embracing my *Gifts of Imperfection*.

Pretty soon, I was flying through a book a week, constructing towers out of the books piled next to my bed. I had become what Sarah Wilson described so well – a soul nerd.

For the spectator in the bleachers, it must have looked like I had become possessed by a ravenous literary monster on a strict non-fiction diet. I had a desperate need to understand myself from the inside out, pursuing the answers with a relentless curiosity.

Scattered amongst the hundreds of thousands of words I devoured, were light bulb moments highlighted in neon. My favourite books, offering a kaleidoscope of colour as I fanned through the pages when I finished each one.

The biggest thrill was feeling the information sticking like Velcro to my brain. It wasn't flying through the flailing hands of my concentration, in one ear and out the other. This time, my brain was grabbing it square in the catcher's mitt with two hands. Each catch, adding to the giant game of dot-to-dot it seemed to be playing up there, joining my past experiences and triggering my comprehension of how the heck I ended up broken, on Jo's red leather couch.

My Beautiful Mess

The more dots I joined, the more I understood. The more I understood, the more I accepted the necessity for change.

My local book shop became my little nook of happiness - call it Willie Wonka's Chocolate Factory of books. As I enthusiastically pushed through the swinging glass door, rather than the wafting aroma of baked cacao, I'd draw the strong scent of freshly printed paper into my lungs. With each step forward, I could feel the tension in my face relax. By the time I'd bypassed the cook books and dodged the human statues fanning through fiction, someone had switched my internal dimmer to a warm glow. My watch may as well had been standing still, as I readied myself to become lost in the depths of non-fiction.

My senses grounded me in that moment. Locking the rest of the world out, even Irene. What I hadn't realised, was that by digesting the authors words from the many books I was reading, Irene's voice had gradually become very quiet, almost a whisper. It was like she had fallen asleep, providing a welcome reprieve.

Jo always said, this "mess" wouldn't last forever. We didn't know how long it would last, but there would be an end in sight and in a bubble of happiness one Wednesday morning in my bookstore, I felt like that first glimmer of hope had caught my eye.

It was a taste of freedom, like I was emerging from hibernation in a deep, dark cave, spying the bright sunlight gleaming through the narrow crack of an entrance. If I am honest with myself, I think I was always cautiously optimistic I would emerge from those shadowed months. Persistence and perseverance were in my blood. I felt like an athlete determined not to fail.

> I will let the gods set the pace. It can be as slow as it likes, but so long as I keep myself moving, I know I'll get there.

Peta Sitcheff

My game has always been the slow game.

If a sales career was a professional sporting event, I'd be an endurance athlete setting a steady pace that would go the distance. I'd never give up.

That Wednesday morning in the bookshop, I knew this was within reach. I was rounding the bend. My world becoming dotted with the colour of freedom. It was a small taste of life without the debilitating shackles of anxiety around my ankles.

Its comfort made me smile.

> It's ok Peta, you are used to the slow burn, you've got this in the bag.

Recommended Reading
-

Tiny Habits
"The Small Changes That Change Everything"
BJ Fogg PhD
Published by Penguin Random House UK (2019)

The Leader Who Had No Title
"A Modern Fable on Finding Real Success in Business and in Life"
Robin Sharma
Published by Simon & Schuster UK Ltd (2010)

This One Wild and Precious Life
"A Hopeful Path Forward in a Fractured World"
Sarah Wilson
Published by Pan MacMillan Australia (2020) p. 31, 157.

The Monk Who Sold His Ferrari
Robin Sharma
Published by HarperElement (2004)

Peta Sitcheff

Truth Bomb
-

"Meeting wonderful people is luck, keeping them in your life takes thought, care, forgiveness and devotion."

Julia Baird

It was easy to see how the inexpensive but powerful human necessity of emotional connection was gobbled up amongst the rigour of the corporate and medical worlds. When I reflect upon the alchemised universe I used to step through, I realise how prone I was to forgetting objective clinical measures, sales figures and diagnostic MRI images, didn't have a heartbeat. Dealing with them day in and day out, could discreetly coat you in Teflon, causing your emotions to slide onto the betadine stained, linoleum floor rather than being absorbed by your starving soul, desperate to be fed.

My Beautiful Mess

For years I had squeezed myself dry of the effort required to build relationships. Work absorbed the lot, leaving dregs in my fuel tank for the rest. It became easier to be on my own. "I prefer my own company anyway," I'd try to unconvincingly remind myself on a sunny Sunday afternoon when the pub was beckoning.

As anyone living on their own would know, you are on a backfoot from the start.

"As a nomad, single parent or widower, you must wake up each day writing your own guidebook for connection and security, and then hustle for it," Sarah Wilson writes in her recent book *This One Wild and Precious Life*. But my hustling power was dwindling and along with it, my confidence.

I could no longer avoid the obvious. While the cocoon of my own company was safe, it kept me trapped in my own head. It was lonely and the antidote to that loneliness, was human connection.

I was back standing on the edge, faced with another mountain to climb.

As I untangled the yarn of my old ways with Jo, unravelling a mindset knotted by preconceived ideas, a profound revelation emerged.

After years of telling myself and believing I was "no good at personal relationships", I was struck by the reality that in fact, I'd been feeding myself a lie all along.

"You're a champion at building trusted professional relationships. What stops you doing this in your personal life?"

It was another red leather couch epiphany. Jo's words ringing in my ears as each syllable ricocheted off my ear drums.

"What is stopping you?"

Peta Sitcheff

I was lost for words. Jo was right. The only thing that was stopping me, was me. Here I had been (not so elegantly) strolling down the path of life and now I lay face down, grazed kneed and sprawled out on the pavement after tripping over an obvious truth I didn't see coming. A truth that until now, my life had camouflaged from view. Of course, Jo was right.

"How the hell have I missed it?" I thought, embarrassed by how oblivious I had been to something that should have been as plain as the maternally inherited nose on my face.

There had always been an undercurrent of awkwardness with my personal relationships. Not the relationship itself, I loved my friends and family. It was more the "doing" of the relationship. I always felt like I would be a nuisance. I think back to that first job interview when I sat there thinking, "Why would a surgeon ever ring me? What could I tell them that they didn't already know?" The personal version of that was "I need a reason to call", "I don't want to interrupt them" or "why would they want to hear form me?" If I didn't have good reason, I wouldn't.

In some cases, I just couldn't. I'd spend all day with this tug of war going on in my head.

> Peta just do it.

I'd go to pick up the phone.

> No Peta, you'll be a nuisance. They'll be in the middle of kid mayhem.

And I'd find an excuse to back out. In the end I would just give it away. The anxiety it provoked was paralysing, and wasted hours in my day.

It never occurred to me, that I didn't need a reason. That someone might just

My Beautiful Mess

appreciate a call to say I was thinking of them in that moment. Connecting emotionally when I couldn't be there in person. If it didn't suit them, it was their choice not to pick up the phone. I didn't have telepathy. I couldn't read their minds. All I had to worry about was the gesture of giving, not the conditions of receiving that I couldn't control. There was no IOU attached to communication.

That was when the penny dropped. It wasn't about what I said at all. It was about how I made people feel. That one sentence spoken by Jo, totally changed the way I viewed relationships.

I'm ashamed to admit that for years, I just assumed the most important people in my life would always be there because they had to be, until they weren't, like Dad. When the people we love are gone, the bookend "The End" is automatically printed. We don't get a choice or an opportunity to write any more chapters of that relationship. I wish I could be gifted with more time to change those adjectives I would use to describe that father daughter bond, but that book is now published, filed in my memory bank.

Fortunately, I still have plenty of chapters to write in relationships that I no longer take for granted. Unconditional relationships where the feelings of love and gratitude are mutual and reciprocated.

That's where my mindset and behaviour had to shift gears.

I started asking rather than telling.
I'd listen with intently rather than distraction.
I'd remember what they said rather than forget.
I'd learn before I would judge.
I'd be patient rather than preoccupied.
I would give rather than take.
It would become about them, not me.

Peta Sitcheff

Lastly, I would give graciously and generously without expectation of return.

I would be selfless.

Recommended Reading
-

The Book of Beautiful Questions
"The Powerful Questions that Will Help you Decide, Create, Connect and Lead"
Warren Berger
Published by Bloomsbury Publishing (2018)

The Resilience Project
"Finding Happiness through Gratitude, Empathy and Mindfulness"
Hugh Van Cuylenburg
Published by Penguin Random House Australia (2019)

My Beautiful Mess

Peta Sitcheff

Today's Wonder
—

"True quiet is the think tank of the soul"

Gordon Hempton

Crunch, crunch, crunch. The sound of the brittle, dinner plate sized autumn leaves crackled under the tread of my sneakers. I could have been walking on plastic bubble wrap, so sharp was the noise that filtered through the local streets that crispy May Melbourne morning. With my hands stuffed in my pant pockets and puffer jacket zipped up to my neck, I marvelled at the brilliant blue of the sky and the fine morning dew on the grass. Individual droplets glistening like fairy lights in the suns first light. My morning stroll to my favourite café had become a joyous daily ritual that I started looking forward to the moment my head hit the pillow the night before. In the absence of a busy work diary, for a while there, it was my reason for getting out of bed.

My Beautiful Mess

After years of working in sterile, windowless hospital operating rooms, I now couldn't wait for the morning Autumn air to hit my face and fill my lungs. It was a stark contrast to the stale oxygen I would breathe in for hours, behind a synthetic hospital face mask.

Too often, I would arrive at work in the dark and leave in the dark. It was a professional Winter solstice. A relentless indoor working day with only fluorescent hospital lighting to nourish my skin. I realise now, how I had missed the natural wonders of the day, never taking the time to appreciate their beauty. Sure, I had lived through 17 Melbourne Autumns, but for most of those annual seasons, I was dashing from one place to another, totally preoccupied by my thoughts or my "to do" list. That's 17 Autumn exhibitions I let pass me by. When I tore up the free ticket, all because I was too busy ruminating the past or blowing some imaginary problem in the future out of proportion. It would only have taken a few minutes each day, to stop and appreciate the sheer beauty mother nature was offering. A moment to jolt me back into the present, the here and now.

With that chapter now in my archives, I felt as though my world had turned from black and white to a vibrant pantone colour chart. A bit like when Dorothy landed in Oz, the brilliant emerald green of the trees and glowing gold of the yellow brick road, a stark contrast to the black and white, vast wheat plains of Kansas.

I'd stroll to my café each morning, the pompom on my blue beanie clad head bobbing up and down with every step. I felt like I had never experienced a true Autumn season before. The wonder of a brilliantly coloured seasonal leaf in gold, deep crimson or burnt orange. How that colour transformed, almost glowing when the sun and leaf were in perfect alignment, illuminating like a cinematic special effect.

That alignment delivers the epitome of presence. The perfect shape, perfect colour, perfect filter from the sun, but only for a fleeting moment. Timing is everything. A few moments wasted, and we miss it. The show

Peta Sitcheff

has disappeared for another day and we have to wait for tomorrow. I have developed somewhat of an obsession for this wonderous occurrence. Insisting on stopping traffic for that perfect photo (much to the amusement of my teenager), except it isn't the photo I am chasing. It is that split-second moment of presence, of the here and now that grounds me to the earth when I hit that camera button.

If I was lucky on my morning stroll, there would be the lingering smell of burnt redgum in the air, emanating from a local's fireplace, still glowing with embers from the night before. There is something about the smell of woodfire that has always drawn me in like a moth to a flame. It connects me to mother nature, grounding me to the earth, reminding me that the most important moment in life is the here and now.

Like that smoky smell, life doesn't last forever. I count myself incredibly blessed to have been woken up at the age of 41. To have taken a deep breath, closed my eyes and bomb dived into a sea of unknown and a whirlpool of fear. Somehow, I managed to keep myself afloat, even if some days it felt like I was in freefall until some random circumstance catapulted me back to the surface for a gasp of air.

The plan was, there was no plan. Like always, I followed my nose, made the most of every opportunity and if something felt wrong, I backed right off, so powerful was the influence of my gut instinct. If something felt right, my curiosity would lead the way like a detective, until it uncovered a clue that would determine my next move.

Without doubt, the necessity for nature in my life has become loud and clear. Its influence is cleansing. It grounds me where I am in that particular moment in time, lifting the fog and distilling my thoughts. It allows me to leave my anxious residue behind and encourages my thoughts to flow freely. There are no whirlpools. Only beautiful free flowing streams.

I recall a wintry afternoon, when I took a spontaneous drive to be with my

My Beautiful Mess

beautiful sister and her family in their country holiday home. On the drive there is a certain west facing hill latticed with grapevines, that as soon as I pass, leaves the city in my wake. The tension in my shoulders dissipates and the smile emerges across my face. With any luck, there is a great 80's song on the radio to sing along to. If ever I was going to belt out a tune on my own, it would be then.

Meandering down the unsealed road to their home is like entering a meditative estate. The gum trees line the roads, pairs of king parrots glide from tree to tree and if you are lucky, you might spy an echidna waddling across the dirt road. It's my idea of heaven.

Afternoons around the fire pit with a glass of locally made red wine are frequent during these visits this one, no exception. I found myself on my own that afternoon, the firepit burning, wafting fresh smoke across the yard. I was drawn to the afternoon sun at the back of the property. There was a small orchard there and a fence leading to a paddock below. Beyond the paddock, stood an army of burnt out trees. It was a gumtree forest destroyed earlier in the year by summer bushfires. The fire decimated any greenery at the time, eucalyptus oil fuelling its rage. From afar, rows of towering blackened tree trunks remained, stripped of their bark, bleak, lifeless and emanating death.

Drawn to the blackened soldiers, I walked across the lush green paddock. Rays from the afternoon sun shot a glimmering reflection off the hardened sap, dripping from the wounds on their trunks, scarred from their bushfire induced trauma months before. Stepping from the paddock into the burnt-out forest was like walking from one palatial room into another. The paddock, a luxe palette of greenery, decorated with shades of jade, lined with a thick shagpile of forest green carpet. Stepping into the burnt-out forest of gums, saw the lush carpet replaced by a Winter damp floor of soggy black leaves offering a spongy feeling underfoot. The décor minimalist, every advancing step strengthening the earthy scent of decomposing leaves. The foliage floor covering was at the end of its life, morphing into nourishment amongst the soil, waiting to be sucked up by the roots of a healing tree to trigger the circle

Peta Sitcheff

of life all over again.

On my own, amongst the gums, I closed my eyes and sucked in the woody air. A whip bird's unique call pierced the silence around me echoing through the valley. There were no leaves for the wind to rustle, no manmade noises to disturb the moment. Only blissful silence.

As I opened my eyes and looked down, I was drawn to flourishing splashes of colour I had failed to see. Through the blackened ground, had speared single blades of brilliant green.

Not only that, the tree trunks had sprouted tiny, tufts of green growth. Fresh shoots bursting through charcoaled, gnarly skin, desperate to drink in the nourishing sunlight. It was Mother Nature yet again reminding us, that with trauma and discomfort, comes new life. Growth.

Suddenly, I realised there were new shoots sprouting everywhere. I had been so mesmerised by the blackened shapes, I had failed to see the new life brimming on the surface.

It was life after burnout.

The metaphor almost knocked the breath out of me, sending shivers up my spine. Here I was, standing in the middle of a burnt-out forest bursting with new life, almost 12 months to the day when my life fell apart. 12 months since I too had burnt out, a hollow shell of my former self remaining. I had to sit in my charcoaled mess, nourish my soul and wait for the new shoots to flourish.

The work had to be done from the inside out, not the outside in. There was no use in polishing the outside in designer clothes to reflect the highlight of a social media reel if the inside was lifeless, hollow and in turmoil. That never worked.

My Beautiful Mess

As my emotional and spiritual health were revived, my mental and physical health followed suit. My brittle, dull hair replaced by a think, glossy blonde mop. Inner calm proving more effective than any fancy hair treatment I could have brought.

I now woke up feeling well rested, not with a thick fog in my head and veil of tiredness over my eyes. Each morning I felt genuinely happy with exactly where I was in that moment instead of going through the motions feeling lifeless and absent of any hope that life could be different.

The connection I felt to my surroundings in that moment was like a shot of adrenalin in my arm, an invigorating validation.

> I'm winning this fight. I'm doing this. Holy smokes, I am happy.

In that afternoon moment, a psychosomatic wave of happiness flooded my body. It was as though every thought in my brain was being released from captivity, like a dense flock of birds, discovering their newly found freedom, spilling into the sky. It felt so surreal, almost like I was floating away with them.

I was experiencing what it was like to be totally out of my head instead of being trapped in its confines looking for the escape hatch. It was similar to a newly found freedom I had discovered through creating, the feeling I was connected with something purposeful and far greater than myself.

For months, I had been toying with the idea of grown up writing, creating proper articles for other peoples eyes. I found the process of writing cathartic and while I didn't know how or what I was going to do with anything I wrote, I knew the way it made me feel would mean it would have to play a part in my life somewhere, I'd work out the "how" later.

It all started some months before, when I felt compelled to capture my burnout story. I couldn't tell you why, it just instinctively felt like something I had to do. Nothing about the process felt difficult or forced. The words just flowed from my brain to my fingertips appearing on my laptop screen as I typed. Next thing I knew, my story was real. It was as though it had vacated my body as I typed, decompressing my brain, taking with it the burden of its secrets and replacing them with the freedom of relief. I had tied a bow around that chapter.

To read the words was exciting and slightly terrifying. I could feel a wave of familiar anxious thoughts bubbling away.

> What will other people think? You put this out there Peta and there is no going back.

While I was happy to own this story, I wasn't yet ready to share this with the world. Feeling more comfortable tucking it safely away in a personal folder on my desktop until the time was right. How would I know when that time was? I had no idea.

On that day in the burnt forest, I knew. It was that time.

I was overcome by an explosion of energy, realising exactly what I had to do next. Knowing no photo would ever do it justice, I did my best to capture the moment with my iPhone, creating a necessary snapshot for what I was about to do.

I flew back across the paddock like a gazelle, my long legs hurdling over the fence, desperate to get my hands on my laptop. Snapping the lid open, I pounded the keys with my password and headed straight to my personal folder. There it was. "My Story."

> Here goes.

I copied the story onto a global blog. Adding to the story the photo I had just taken, I sent it off to the editor without hesitation, comforted by the fact it

My Beautiful Mess

was not yet published and still hidden from public view.

> Hell, I'll have a week or so at least before I hear back and if it's published, I'll deal with it then.

Not quite. I woke the next morning, taking a few seconds to remember where my brain left off the night before. I threw back the bedcovers and grabbed my laptop. Opening it to check for my article's status, "Published".

> Shit! How did that happen so quickly?

Sure enough, when I looked it up there I was, totally exposed in public view. I could feel a wave of anxious prickles mounting across my skin and I started drawing deep slow breaths to bring perspective back to the situation.

> Peta calm the heck down. No one is looking for this, it's in a tiny corner of the internet. Not an aerial banner jetting across Melbourne CBD for god's sake.

My brain was defaulting to panic, galloping away from reality (picture Irene on a white horse, hurtling across a green field, purple cloak flying behind her), lured by the temptation to make more of this than it needed to.

> Rational thoughts, Peta.

A side from the article, absolutely nothing else had changed from yesterday, this was my head in its drama queen costume, I reminded myself.

Months ago, this would have crippled me with paranoia for weeks. "What would people think?" in purple neon lighting up and flashing in my brain. There was something very satisfying that for now, this wasn't the case. The only person whose opinion mattered was my own and I knew I was coming from a genuine position of wanting to help other people by sharing my story.

Peta Sitcheff

With that comfort, it didn't take long for my brain to catch up with my runaway emotions. I was able to get on with my day happily in the knowledge that "My Story" was still tucked away, even if that corner was on global blog and no longer only on my laptop.

After 24 hours, I ripped off that band aid, taking with it a few prickly anxious hairs and published it on my social media accounts. It's difficult to describe the feeling. The initial feeling of freedom I felt when I moved the words from my head to the page months earlier, was nothing compared to the exhilaration that came with sharing it with the world. It wasn't so much a feeling of closure, which months earlier, I would have expected. This was a feeling of acceptance. Of accepting responsibility for decisions I had made and acknowledging all I had been learning from this incredible chapter in my life.

I also felt brave. Brave that I wasn't afraid of sharing my story. Of turning myself inside out and exposing my vulnerabilities. More of us need to share our real stories instead of constantly trying to keep up appearances and fuel perceptions that may no longer accurately reflect our intentions.

It is these biases that create the pressure that crack people's wellbeing like a piece of fine English porcelain dropped on a polished concrete floor. It was freeing myself from the speculation of others by filling in the gaps myself. I was sharing my story in the hope it might help one other person in this universe from getting themselves into the tangled mess of a life I had just spent 12 months unravelling. To that end, it sure did.

"I can totally relate to your words."

"I have a feeling you will understand me."

"I'm so lost."

The sentiments flowed. I could feel the emotion connecting me through the

My Beautiful Mess

words to the people who reached out. Some with niggles, others who were standing right on a cliff's edge and needed guidance towards professional support.

Through the process of creation, had emerged a purpose I not only identified with, but I desperately wanted to master. These were the people I wanted to serve. How could I offer my best to serve them well? It wouldn't be about having all of the answers. Rather, being able to offer a safe space to sit, a focused ear that would listen and a mind that had been there before to relate in some capacity.

Of all of the sentiments I received, there was one that struck a deep emotional cord. It was a moment that made me feel the 13 years was worth it, after a good 12 months of feeling it was worth nothing.

It was a note from The Director after he had read the article.

"I had no idea what you were going through and if in any way I or we did anything to contribute or make matters worse, I am deeply sorry. By the way, I would have smashed that frame too."

Finally, the bow was tied around that chapter.

The words made me feel human.

Peta Sitcheff

Today's Reflection
-

The moment we realise the mounting fear within us won't go away, is a moment to embrace. To understand it is real and that what is important to us, matters.

As isolating as it can feel, no one needs to wander through this journey alone. Support is all around us, but it does mean we need to take the first step and ask for help. Remember, other people can't read our minds.

Hope is in front of us, along with its best friend "choice", even if for now, we can't see it through the dense fog of confused emotions that cloud our view. Just know they are there, patiently waiting until the time is right.

Recommended Reading
—

Braving the Wilderness
"The Quest for True Belonging and the Courage to Stand Alone"
Brené Brown
Published by Penguin Random House UK (2017)

The Surrender Experiment
"My Journey To Life's Perfection"
Michael A. Singer
Published by Yellow Kite Books (2016)

Peta Sitcheff

Lewis

―

"You can have it all, just not all at the same time"

Dame Quentin Bryce

I watch as Lewis wolfed down his steaming crepes drowned in amber maple syrup, with a smile of total delight. I can't help but cast my mind back to the times where he sucked his breakfast through a thick red and white straw, a barber shop pole sticking out of a domed plastic cup. We would leave home at 7.05am. Some mornings it would be in such a flurry it was like the house vomited us out the door. I would speed dial the local cafe as I started the car ignition and order our liquid breakfast ahead of time. Collection at 7.10am. If we heard the 7.12am morning quiz on the FM radio on the way there, we were late. Damn.

My kiddo's sleepy eyes always lit up as I emerged from the café, banana smoothie in one hand, latte in the other. He would happily slurp away, the cup empty by our 7.15am drop off at before school care. His was always the first name scrawled across the top of the list.

By 7.17am, I'd be driving on autopilot to the hospital, working my way through

My Beautiful Mess

a labyrinth of a switchboard, to gauge the lay of the land for the day ahead. There was always a 50/50 chance it would be different to what it was when I checked 9pm the night before. Such was the revolving world. If my 8am case happened to be cancelled, my late Nan would wash my mouth out with soap so colourful was the language that would echo around my car cabin after hanging up the phone. All that rush for nothing. Cursing, I'd turn the car around and head home.

There are no words to describe how happy I am to leave that morning pressure cooker in another life. In comparison, today's teenage mornings are best described as a slow cook simmer. We rise without the unwelcome intervention of any shrill alarm, our bodies and minds well rested and ready for the day ahead. The morning is calm, as is my brain. It welcomes the luxury of space it has been afforded, relishing in newly paved neural pathways, illuminated by inspired creative thoughts.

The new relaxed pace has given my brain the opportunity to heal from 15 years of reality I had swept under the carpet. To relearn how to function using its entire capacity rather than singeing its edges through a constant state of emotional reactivity.

It's a brain that is happy where it is, not desperately wishing it was somewhere it wasn't.

As for Lewis, he and I are a team. As thick as thieves. Our heads synchronised as we work together to get the household going for the day. No longer is one of us dragging the other out the door.

It feels almost overnight the young child has faded away, replaced by a gentle young man who unwittingly is becoming my protector. With every day that passes and centimetre taller he grows, the nurturer within him evolves. It's a role that appears to come naturally and a responsibility that fits him like a glove.

Peta Sitcheff

Today, we both recognise the words and tones of Irene's voice along with the triggers that turn up the volume on her surround sound. Lewis knows exactly how to stop her in her tracks when she casts an anxious hook.

"Mum, you're obsessing. Stop!" "Don't stress. I've got this," he will say, immediately breaking the unnecessary panic circuit roaring in my brain. I stand there stunned by the intelligence of his awareness and the effectiveness of his words. He is right. I'm not helping. He is doing his maths test not me. He knows what is best for him and his brain now. I have to let go, accept his reassurance and offer my trust.

I couldn't be prouder as he demonstrates wisdom well beyond his 14 years, separating my anxious behaviour from me the person. The reality that the three of us can coexist is a blessing.

Relentlessly curious, I recently I had one of my light bulb moments at home, grabbing Lewis, his teenage enthusiasm and a rainbow block of post-it notes. Together, we completed what I can only describe as an intimate moment of truth.

With a line down the middle of a poster board, blue tacked onto my European laundry door, I asked Lewis if he would be happy to share how he felt within himself and how he would describe me, before and after I had left my job. I reassured him he had free reign – "say what you like, be honest, there is no right or wrong here. I will respect everything you say." I was going to do the same from my perspective. His post-it notes were pink, mine were yellow – and did he paint the board pink. He let rip. Pink notes were slapped left, right and centre with gusto. His handwritten words "angry", "hard" and "never listen" staring me in the face, impossible to hide from.

We have a mantra in our family, we keep talking. There are no wrong questions or bad questions, we don't avoid hard conversations and secrets, they are left for the squirrels. I have always found the more honest and adult I have been in conversation, the more Lewis has risen to the occasion

My Beautiful Mess

and genuinely empathised. Often, pointing out I might be overcomplicating things. You think?!

Kids sure do keep it simple and sometimes, simple is best.

This was one of the reasons I made the decision to share my mental health journey with Lewis. With only two of us in the household, I couldn't hide what I was going through, nor did I want to. More than ever, I needed to be me. Stripped back, warts and all. Not hide from the person I had been avoiding, Irene. That is what got me into this mess to start with.

He needed to know Irene was nothing to be afraid of and more important to me, he needed to be assured his Mum was always going to be honest with him - keep talking.

Despite our household always looking a little different from the traditional Mum, Dad and two kids, we have always done our best to emphasise to the little guy we are one family. He has one family that loves him unconditionally. It just so happened that what was best for us, was for Mum and Dad to live separately.

"Families come in all shapes and sizes" we've always said trying to highlight the normality of change within today's evolving world. Despite these efforts, there were still blind spots that would slip between the cracks.

I remember when he was only six or seven, he casually dropped into conversation over a very crumbly muffin that he "didn't have a home."

Trying not to spit out my latte and let the rising inside panic show in my face. What should have come out as, "What do you mean darling?" was more of a stunned "Huh?!"

"Well, I have your house and Dad's house, but not my house," he said innocently.

Peta Sitcheff

It took a few moments for the words to sink in. Here he was happily devouring his sweet delight in front of me and there I was, feeling like I had been struck by an unexpected parenting meteorite, splattering my emotions across the café floor. The thought of him not identifying with a home absolutely gutted me.

Where have I gone wrong? I've failed. Christ, he doesn't feel loved.

The anxious hooks were thrown left, right and centre.

"Breathe Peta," I muttered under my breath.

When I slowed my churning mind and put myself into his six year old shoes for a minute, I cast my mind back to routine weekly conversations. He was right. He was always going to Dad's house or Mum's house. Never his house.

From that moment, language had to change. "We have one family and two houses, both are your home - no more Dad's house or Mum's house"

The South Melbourne house and Port Melbourne house it was. I always like to think it is a giant rainbow of love for Lewis that unites the two.

That's the way we have rolled for almost ten years now. It is our normal. We make every family decision together, celebrate festivities together and Lewis has always come first. We keep talking. What happens in one house happens in the other. Has it always been easy? Of course not, separation is heartbreaking. The initial days, weeks and months when your child isn't under your roof is horrible. Your heart feels as empty as the house itself. There is no point in trying to dress it up. It's a shit time.

As a parent, you have to believe in the bottom of your heart, that you are doing what is best. That if you are happy, your kiddo will be happy. Some of the best advice I was ever given; accept your relationship with your kids

My Beautiful Mess

is going to be different from that moment. Not worse, different. I can say with 100% confidence, this is true and mine is better. We have worked hard at that and I have no doubt, the strength of respect his Dad Troy and I have always had for each other, is what has kept us buoyant through the initial turbulence.

It's been fascinating observing Lewis as the years have gone by. He is now old enough to appreciate the relationship Troy and I have worked so hard to foster. He understands and has seen that not all kids from separated households are in the same position.

This rang true a few years ago when in between properties Troy came to stay for a week. On the first night, as we all ventured to bed, our separate rooms in a row. The lights went out and I got the usual, "Night Mum!" down the hallway. This time, "Night Dad!" followed. After a few seconds silence: "Guys, this is really weird!" Our laughs echoed up the hallway in the darkness. I remember smiling to myself and thinking, our kiddo is just fine.

I was a few years down the track from sitting in my mess then. We had all settled into a happier life with room to breathe. There were still wobbly days, but we had found our groove and with what I felt he could handle, I had shared them in a language I felt he could understand.

This meant introducing Irene to the household, rather than keep her in the confines of Jo's office, a stranger he would never get to know. He didn't need more mental absence, he needed the comforting embrace of familiarity and connection.

Always dance with the elephant I say.

Interestingly, when I was initially introducing him to Irene and her quirks, he said he understood.

"What do you mean?" I curiously asked at the same time thinking "crikey,

Peta Sitcheff

there's an old soul in there!"

"I get storms in my brain too. When I feel silly for feeling so scared about something, but I don't know how to stop being afraid. Like camp."

I was gobsmacked. My 10 year old son knew exactly what I meant when I said it felt like there was a storm in my head, because unbeknownst to me, he had experienced it too. Where I had struggled to explain how I felt for so long, he articulated it beautifully in 10 seconds.

Allow me to introduce you to Boris.

For years, Lewis had tip toed around me, looking for reassurance and ways to connect with a Mum who was constantly distracted. He wanted security and I wasn't giving it to him. As a result, the smallest things overwhelmed him and sent him into a spiral of emotional negativity that was impossible to stop. It all made sense.

Four years ago, we were both burnt out and needed rewiring.

And that is what we did. I became the Mum who was there.

I had the time and patience to help with homework and when I could see he was wobbly, I would calmly work through it with him, reassuring him I understood how he was feeling. As Jo reminded me, who better to show him how to manage his wobbly ground than someone who had been through it herself? Me.

When these episodes cropped up, we no longer put them between us like a battlefield, we put them in front of us, linked arms and calmly stepped through them together.

Back to the sea of "post-it" pink.

My Beautiful Mess

On the left, words like - "scared, lonely, never home and pissed off," have been replaced by - "calm, happy, listens to me and home more often" on the right. Two particular notes that needed some explanation were one with the name of my old company on the left, and one with my surname "Sitcheff", on the right.

"What's this buddy?" I asked.

"For ages I thought that was your surname Mum, because that was how you used to answer the phone. Now I know it's not, because you don't answer the phone that way anymore".

I was stunned.

Now he is a bit older and we have anchored ourselves to terra firma, we regularly chat about what's important to us. Household decisions are exactly that, household decisions. Not individual decisions. We have created boundaries defining "what is" and "what isn't ok" in his home, across both houses.

Our priority - presence and connection. Neither of us are any good when we isolate ourselves. What's good for the goose is good for the gander.

No phone for him, no phone for me. Dedicated individual time and dedicated together time. We make time for talking so he understands my world and I understand his. Curiosity is welcomed - there are no wrong questions. If you don't ask, you don't know the facts, if you don't know the facts, you can't truly understand. It goes both ways. We put judgement aside and we don't partake in the "blame game".

If one of us is feeling sorry for ourselves, the other lifts their chin with a gentle reminder that for every cup half empty is another half full. He knows I am proud of him and equally, he shares with me when he feels pride in my achievements. "How did your meeting go today Mum?" or "Awesome Mum,

Peta Sitcheff

well done on that new client." Sharing our successes makes my heart swell.

It's a true partnership in every sense of the word, in good times and in bad. I have realised, my journey is his journey too.

Of course, this doesn't run on script every day. He is now a teenager and I go through hormonal waves of emotion. Our shared DNA sees us lock horns on daily realities, like towels on the floor and gaping cupboard doors and every now and then we need to air the closet with a good row over something totally trivial. Generally, it ends up with us both laughing and blaming Irene or Boris.

Only once in the past year has he had to give me a dose of truth with a smack in the guts. As much as it hurt my insides at the time, I was grateful and proud of him for speaking up. Juggling dinner, homework and a tired brain I was short and distracted for the first time in ages.

"Mum, you are being just like you were back THEN!"

Ouch. I shudder at the thought of him describing his childhood with me as the post-it notes on the left. I look back and realise how difficult it must have been for him to understand his own mother when I didn't even understand myself.

Any wonder he knows me so well.

Not once did he give up on me. He didn't rebel, act up or make judgement. He kept trying. Trying to reach out and connect, determined to knit our little family back together and wrap himself in the warm homely blanket we both craved.

Thankfully, we now share that load and knit away together.

Recommended Reading
-

More Than A Woman
Caitlin Moran
Published by Penguin Random House UK (2020)

Peta Sitcheff

Joy
-

"Remember you cannot go anywhere if you have not imagined yourself there...that which you have never dreamed of, is that which you will never attain."

John Bertrand AO

On November 5th 2019 I was celebrating more than my 44th birthday. It was a celebration of survival, persistence and belief in myself. There I stood, on the perimeter of the iconic Flemington racecourse parade ring. Framed by its legendary blossoming yellow roses, the air electric with the pomp and circumstance deserving only for its grandest show of the year. It was exactly as I imagined.

We were within minutes from the start of the "race that stops the nation." The Melbourne Cup. The tension within the mounting yard palpable, as owners and their families anxiously paced the cordoned off square, each hoping it

My Beautiful Mess

would be their thoroughbred's nose that crossed the finish line first. The prize money handsome, but the prestige, priceless.

One amongst the 86 000 strong crowd, I tried to suck as much of the incredible atmosphere into my lungs as I could. The rainbow of bright jockey silks sparkling in the mid-afternoon sun. The exquisite millinery upon the groomed heads of women. Feathers, leathers and bows crafted into stunning pieces of wearable contemporary art. The spectacle of the magnificent equine athletes, their musculature pulsing in anticipation for the moments ahead. The notes of the national anthem echoing around the track and ringing in my ears.

Feeling totally overwhelmed with exhilarated emotion, I remember warning myself; "don't lose your noodle Peta, you are working with the Victorian Racing Club", thankful my tinted Tom Fords were hiding my eyes, brimming with happy tears. How embarrassing. I'm always a sook when live music is involved, it gets into my bones. It's my gauge of a good show, my bawling intensity.

For two years, I'd rearranged my entire relationship with myself and decided rather than settling on a fixed picture for my professional future, I would throw caution to the wind and see where that weather pattern blew me. With my values as my compass, my rate of progress determined by my level of curiosity. It might have been a path in a dense jungle that needed a machete to clear the way, but that was me. I was my happiest in the unchartered territory everyone else avoided. For the first time in a long while, I had fire in my belly for the chase. This time, the product I was selling, was me.

I'd tied a bow around one magnificent professional chapter that through its challenges, offered a PhD in life. Now I was living another and while I knew it wouldn't be easy, I didn't think for a second, I wouldn't get there.

Even if I wasn't really sure where "there" was. I was strangely comfortable with not knowing.

Peta Sitcheff

My coaching business was back up and running, with a stable of grateful private clients. An emerging trend of interest, coming from puzzled individuals traversing their own career ravines. The feeling of being drawn down this purposeful path was visceral. I could tell it was leading me somewhere. I never would have thought that "somewhere" was the words on these pages.

Managing my inner racehorse, I sought to balance out my support of others with some individual pursuit designing and chasing commercial growth. That was to be my formula to professional fulfillment. I didn't need the answers immediately. Jo was controlling the reins of that race. All I knew was I was being drawn to opportunities that would bring out my best and where I felt could make a real impact.

It was my first public outing post anxiety diagnosis and I hadn't gone small – Presidents Table at the Collingwood vs Geelong AFL match at the infamous Melbourne Cricket Ground. I felt like a tiny, fragile bird stepping into a sea of confident suits.

> Avoid the eyes and find your seat Peta.

Raw memories of my previous corporate lunch escapade rising to the surface. I was determined not to end up on the concrete floor of a carpark today.

I had no idea how I would go striking up a conversation with strangers, but I needn't have worried. Relief filtered through my limbs as I spied my cursive name printed on a place card at the end of the long table of 20. As I went to take my seat, an outstretched hand and a warm smile by the woman sitting opposite me put me at ease straight away. Clearly, she did this often. "Hi, I'm Rasa." As I shook her hand. Soon we were chatting like old friends and I was reminded by how much I enjoyed meeting new people who cared enough to listen. I felt her kindness. She asked what I did, my response rehearsed and ready to go, "I've taken some time out to spend with my son and work out what's next."

My Beautiful Mess

"Tell me about your boy." Always a gushy Mum, I could feel the smile on my face and sparkle in my eyes. I never tire of talking about my love. We went on to chat about my passion for coaching and for supporting young women through professional change when she politely interrupted and said, "You need to meet my husband, John" as she tapped the tall man behind her on the shoulder.

"John, I want you to meet Peta. I think you will get on well."

And there over a plate of kingfish ceviche, I was introduced to John Bertrand. Skipper of the winning yacht in the 1983 America's Cup, an experienced navigator of the wildest of seas, a leader who knew how to read the play and a skipper who could extract the best out of his crew. He was a leader who dreamed of winning, who visualised the finish line and brought everyone with him, along for the ride. He delivered.

If only he knew he was being introduced to someone who had been bobbing aimlessly through the sea of life for the past year with all the elegance of a two year old flapping in her bright yellow floaties.

The good news, was that finally, I was beginning to visualise my own finish line.

In the last few red couch sessions with Jo, I had toyed with the idea of exploring opportunities in high-performance industries where I could be plonked in the middle of a confusing tangle of total chaos and let my hyper-alertness go to work. Rapidly moving landscapes that would offer my explorer brain the constant challenge of unchartered waters and surround me with inspiring high-performance minds. This meeting seemed somewhat serendipitous.

Some of my fondest childhood memories were of my yachting mad Pop, sitting in his green carpeted Jason recliner watching the start of the Sydney to Hobart yacht race every Boxing Day (also his birthday), without fail. I knew exactly who John was and desperately tried not to be overwhelmed by his presence.

> Pull yourself together woman.

I discreetly eyed the door of the lady's room in the back corner, just in case a quick getaway was necessary.

I had to block out the layers of crowd noise to not set off Irene's trip meter. We had been getting along so well, to the point where I now felt a strange urge to protect her from her own sporadic impulses.

Feeling desperate, I delved frantically into my mental toolbox. Embracing my coaching skills, I regulated my breathing, in for four, out for four, and honed in on our conversation. I joined his syllables into words and strung the words into sentences. It was working. Phew.

I was smiling on the inside, everyone around me, including John, oblivious to the significance of this moment. I could feel the dry water beds of my confidence, filling with trickles of water, very slowly coming back to life.

As I explained to John what I was thinking of doing I posed my two predicaments; I need to understand where the opportunities were and how to articulate my value in this new world.

"How can I help?" was his response. As sceptical as I was when I first thought I would ever say anything useful to a surgeon, I was dumbfounded that John Bertrand would offer me his helping hand. I wasn't used to people offering help. Nor was I used to accepting it. What I did know, was the new me needed to accept help from others to start building those bridges. He was graciously offering a gesture which I would graciously receive.

It was a conversation that flicked a switch. If someone like John Bertrand believed this was possible, then that was enough for me. He very generously

My Beautiful Mess

offered introductions he didn't have to. He offered his ear for advice. That he didn't have to do. He said he believed in me. - someone he had only known for a few hours. That he didn't have to do. He made me feel like I could.

It was the way he made me feel, that mattered most.

Today's Reflection
-

That conversation with John, led to many an introduction to people who have offered their valuable time and spirit and shaped the way I view mentorship. They have given generously, received gratefully with no expectation of return. They wanted to help and lift someone who needed a boost.

Investing in building my network has helped me get out of my own way. I've had to confront my fears head on and muster the courage to reach out to people I didn't know with no expectation of return.

All of them, graciously returned.

My lesson, people are kind and want to help. All you have to do is ask.

Recommended Reading
-

It's Who you Know
"How a Network of 12 Key People Can Fast-track Your Success"
Janine Garner
Published by John Wiley & Sons Australia Ltd (2017)

Born to Win
"The Power of a Vision"
John Bertrand AO
Published by Sidgwick & Jackson Ltd (1985)
Amazon Fire p. 2796

Mirror Thinking
"How Role Models Make Us Human"
Fiona Murden
Published by Bloomsbury Sigma (2020)

Range
"How Generalists Triumph in a Specialised World"
David Epstein
Published by MacMillan (2019)

My Beautiful Mess

Peta Sitcheff

Boggle Brain
-

"A profound side effect of friendship is gratitude. Gratitude for the opportunity to show vulnerability and still be loved. For the forgiveness of our flawed lives. For the shared trust and time together and the feeling of belonging which is the ultimate glue that holds friends together."

Vivek H. Murthy

"I've got this. I've so got this!" I rejoiced to myself. Irene sat back, nodding her head, clearly thinking ,"Yeah, you do, but don't go getting ahead of yourself missy." I knew better than to ignore the cautionary words of this wise woman.

We had landed in a good place, Irene and I. After months on Jo's red leather couch, we had finally learnt to demystify each other's ways. Slowly, knitting together a healthy partnership bound by gentle mutual respect. It was a

My Beautiful Mess

vast contrast to the wild ride of the past when my fear set the pace. The antagonistic, slinging matches of old were replaced by a dialogue between two souls that often surprised me with its level of maturity.

"When did we become so bloody sensible?" I'd think to myself, marvelled by our progress.

I had been rolling through life in a comfortable, rhythmic cadence for some time. Cruising through the days, exactly what I needed to appreciate this sweet spot of still content. For once, I wasn't in any rush to find "my next big thing." Instead, I was content idling through the months like a British racing green convertible motoring through the undulating pastures of the picturesque English countryside.

I had done the work on myself and fully understood that work would now never stop. My journey was fuelled by purpose. My compass powered by values. Without the need for the menacingly rigid structure of old, I was now free to allow my mind and spirit to roam like a nomad. To explore the wonders of the universe for the clues that would fuel my growth and lead me to my next opportunity. My next place of purposeful residence.

Gone was the need to control my life like a bacterial cluster in the confines of a petri dish. I could now colour outside the lines and confidently venture into the unchartered waters where I felt most alive. Ah the serenity. Then, in the midst of my drunken, romantic haze of blushing hues and sweeping rainbows, life threw a soggy, stinky sponge straight in my face.

Anxiety had a cruel way of messing with my brain in different ways. Some were obvious, others less so, giving even more reason as to why they should be spoken about. You can't understand what you don't know.

I was reminded of this during a recent group presentation I was giving. In the era of COVID-19, it was on Zoom and fortunately for me, in a psychologically safe space with 25 pairs of kind eyes. Despite having my slides and

Peta Sitcheff

commentary notes beside me, I knew I was in trouble after uttering the first word. My intended opening line had mysteriously vanished from my brain, leaving my mouth scrambling to fill the silence. Between my brain and mouth the words weren't even scrambled, they were lost. Clutching at the first word that jumped out of my commentary notes, I blurted the first handwritten line I could see. One that was reserved for much later in the presentation.

If my mind was a game of boggle, before the presentation I had neatly lined up the words in perfect sequence for my delivery. Then suddenly, someone hijacked them with the Perspex lid and shook the cube violently, as a slick bartender would their finest Tom Collins. Where the letters fell, was the scrambled mess I had to decipher, live on Zoom. With an audience staring at me. One expecting the professionalism I was paid to deliver.

I felt the furnace in my body fire up and my fingers become clammy with perspiration.

"Stop!" my mind yelled, but I pushed on, the barrage of words falling out of my mouth in a language I didn't understand. From the discombobulated faces in the boxes on the screen, I could see it sounded as much like gobbledy-gook as it felt.

Scrambling to resurrect the mess, I started clutching at straws. Handwritten words in the margin of a page, stand out phrases I had highlighted, the book in front of me.

    That will do.

I grabbed the security of my book's pages. Frantically I looked for anchors that would bide me time to steer my brain back onto a smooth, comprehensible bitumen highway. Instead, it stayed in rugged, 4WD terrain.

    You have to stop Pete, otherwise this will steamroll.

My Beautiful Mess

Irene whispered softly, using my nickname for the first time. She must have been concerned. She was right, I had to own this. If I didn't break this circuit, it would get worse before it got better. If it went on at all.

> This is a safe space Peta. These people know you. You've got this.

Stopping myself mid-flight I paused and took a deep breath.

"I'm sorry guys. I'm not well, please give me a minute," I said to the concerned faces in front of me.

I closed my eyes and took a few deep breaths. Looking at the slide in front of me, I slowed my words and posed a question to the group. With enormous gratitude I listened to them start a conversation amongst themselves that I then facilitated. It was the quickest strategy I could come up with to work through the situation and relieve the pressure on my brain. It worked.

As I listened to the banter, all I could think was:

> I have two choices here. Either one, be highly embarrassed and hide forever or two, own this and be proud that I can now manage a situation that in a previous life, would have muzzled me.

I chose the latter.

It was a scenario full of lessons for the wonderful humans on that virtual call. All of whom worked in a values-led, professional environment full of compassion and purpose.

I couldn't have picked a safer space to slide down that slope.

Peta Sitcheff

Recommended Reading
-

The Power of Moments
"Why Certain Experiences have Extraordinary Impact"
Chip Heath & Dan Heath
Published by Penguin Random House UK (2019)

Brave Not Perfect
"Fear Less, Fail More, Live Bolder"
Reshma Saujani
Published by HarperCollins (2020)

My Beautiful Mess

Peta Sitcheff

My Birds
—

> "Sink into yourself, the birds come around and look at you. It's true, they do."
>
> Robert Louis Stevenson

The fear in their beady black eyes shot out like laser beams. I stood with statuesque stillness, my only movement the rise and fall of my heaving breast bone. My warm breath turning to mist as it collided with the crisp Winter air. Slowly, I inched one woollen dressed foot forward on the damp timber decking. Their heads countered my movement and cocked to the side. I couldn't help but wonder what they were thinking.

"Do we trust this tall figure with the fluffy fur pom-pom on her head that is better suited to a rabbits butt?"

    Fair enough.

My Beautiful Mess

"I promise guys, I'm nothing to be afraid of," I muttered to myself.

They had my undivided attention. The only thing that mattered to me in that moment, was earning the trust of my native avian friends. I had nowhere else to be. My muscles no longer housed the tension from the city, my limbs swayed in a smooth adagio, the perfect accompaniment to the classical pace of the day ahead.

The early view of the expansive green valley never failed to take my breath away. Rolling hills dotted with friesian cows, udders burst with dairy goodness anticipating their morning reprieve. Beyond the hills in the distance the white caps of the sea rolled. The menacing navy blue of Bass Strait was a stark contrast from the shallow aqua hues of the tropical north. Instantly, I felt my spirit connecting to its heartbeat, nourishing me with its energy.

My mind felt perfectly still and profoundly connected to that moment. I was hyper aware of my surrounds. The smoky scent of last night's fire lingering in the air, the sharp edges of birdseed rattling around in my closed palm. The drips of morning dew sparkling like diamonds on the barbed wire fence, the pair of rosella lovers chattering to themselves in the towering gum overhead.

This truly was all that mattered. A moment of sublime perfection that I wanted to bottle and tuck away in a pocket close to my heart. Its instruction label, "inhale as directed". After a lifetime of trapped mental confusion, I had found the escape hatch from my own head. One that released the intense storms of rumination and reduced their significance to an indistinguishable ripple on the surface of my day. So too was the medicinal power of Mother Nature.

She had me captivated. The synchronicity of the circles of life that she managed with aplomb. Magically, they dance around one another, occasionally colliding, maybe one shatters. But she always has a plan. She just keeps going, a force unto her own. From burnt out remains springs

Peta Sitcheff

luminescent green growth. From fallen trees, new hiding places emerge for endangered marsupials. The inspiration we can draw from her brilliance, is never ending. The colour palettes that inspire budding artists, the plants that nourish the ill, the tales written from the exploration of her most spectacular wonders.

She is remarkable, powerful and quite simply, I now know I need her in my life. It's not even a want. It's a need, as much as my cells need food and water. My mind relies on her to cleanse its synapses. My soul, dependent on her power to remind me I am but a tiny blot on this earth, forever connected to her expansive universe. I am and will never again, be alone.

Slowly, I trailed birdseed along the timber bannister. My brightly coloured angels spying on me from above. The boldest king hopped down onto a lower branch. Closer, but still a safe distance away. I edged towards the outdoor setting, lowering myself onto its damp seat. Then I waited.

"I'm not going anywhere guys. I've got all day." Finally, the king parrots dropped to the bannister, first him then her. Their red and green feathers were electric against the moss covered wooden timber. You could hear the snap, crackle, pop as they expertly shelled the sunflower seeds, devouring the sweet kernel treasure inside. Clearly there was a pecking order here as the crimson rosellas watched pensively from the neighbouring gum.

Slowly, I stretched out my hand across the table, my palm full of seed.

Minutes went by, then a crimson beauty dropped. One then two. Always in pairs. I sat perfectly still, my fingers outstretched. Closer they nudged, until one finally mustered the courage.

> I know how you feel little guy. Don't worry – I'm here for the long game.

I felt a smile spread across my face as the pitter patter of their beak nibbled against my hand.

Still in my body and still in my mind. They came.

Recommended Reading
-

The Thing Your Think You Cannot Do
"Thirty Truths about Fear and Courage"
Gordon Livingstone, M.D.
Published by Hachette Australia (2012)
p. 183.

Peta Sitcheff

Success
—

"When we are hyper focused on outcome, the human component of how we win gets swept under the rug."

Valorie Kondos Field

If someone asked me today how much it would cost to keep me happy, the answer would be simple. Nothing.

If you had asked me 10 years ago, I would have said half a million dollars a year, but hang on, sometimes that wasn't enough to feed my hungry ego.

I'd stepped out of a life where I'd allowed my happiness to become shallow and expensive, all because I didn't understand the person I was. I hadn't delved into my layers to understand what made me happy or what I stood for once the job title was removed and the accolades stopped flowing. I didn't understand, I was enough.

I had to throw off my protective armour, jump from the mothership without

My Beautiful Mess

a parachute and watch my anxiety splatter from pillar to post, to finally understand this wasn't about my job at all.

This was about me.

This was about me finally understanding that I was the only person who could make me happy. No fancy reward, designer outfit or amount of money, would ever be enough. So long as I continued to look for happiness in the dress up box, the adrenaline would satisfy my appetite for as long as that rush would last, then it would want for more. My mental self would make sense of it and impatiently move on. My emotional self would lap up the feeling for a few moments and then quickly forget as it vanished into the ether. For a long time, I was permanently in a state of fight or flight, too busy reacting to the compromising situations I was throwing it into.

As for my spiritual self, extrinsic reward would never quench the thirst of my soul. Like a sprinkle of summer rain on a dry ground, it could never penetrate deep enough to reach the roots.

I've learnt it wasn't enough to be engaged in my job alone, that one part of my life should never define my whole life.

To be the best version of me, I needed to engage every quadrant of my being. My mind, my body, my spirit and my emotional self. To understand what made my heart race with love, my body connect to the earth, and my brain cells dance with curiosity.

And then there was my neglected spirit.

Like a lighthouse casting a beam of brilliance across a blackened ocean, my spirit had the answers all along. Answers I now see. Gently, it illuminated my path forward, offering a safe direction that would protect its glow from fading.

Peta Sitcheff

To protect its integrity, I'm now regularly held to account, by asking myself the burning question, "What do you stand for today?"

I must answer that question with undying honesty and accept that if I don't, come hell or high water, there will be consequences.

The words that shape that answer, form my personal terms and conditions – what is and is not OK in my world in that moment. It is the fine print I now vow to nurture and protect with the ferocity of a lioness protecting her newly born cubs.

A life led with integrity, would be a life led with honesty to one person, me.

Never again would I dishonour myself.

I could never have integrity when my life existed in a divided state. I wasn't designed to split myself in two. To be radiating happiness on one side of the fence, shrivelled and stale on the other. It broke me in the end.

I live with integrity when my world is meshed together, when all of my versions are integrated and exist as a whole. When my heart and my head are on speaking terms and at least moving in the same direction (even if they aren't quite dancing yet).

Like the tinman, this old robot was always looking for her heart, but was too distracted by numbers in her head to commit to the cause.

Thankfully, I no longer live or die by that sales number. The number I would eagerly wait for each morning at 7.03am, waiting for it to drop at 7.04am. The one message that would program me for the day and determine the type of mother my kiddo would wake up to as the hourglass counted down the frantic minutes to the morning scramble out the door.

My days were spent obsessing on how to increase those numbers to prove I was enough. I'd overshare the hours of my life to deliver the best service, my head preoccupied with concocting my next strategic move. Like Pavlov's dog, the numbers made me work harder, my brain focused on the dollars with each commission milestone that passed. I needed that money to maintain the white-knuckle grip on my security, self-worth and what I thought made me happy.

I was a foot soldier under the eagle eyes of those monitoring, phone at the ready to pose a question if the run rate wasn't up to scratch.

That number and what it represented, was my definition of success. Then.

> *"We can't lead from a place when winning is our only metric of success and when our ego is centre stage. It has been proven that concept produces broken human beings.*
>
> *We can produce trained champions in life, in every walk of life, without compromising the human spirit. That starts with redefining success"*
>
> Valorie Kondos Field

Today at 7.04am I was strength training my body and stilling my mind. Breathing its benefits as it woke up my muscle fibres, charging them with energy for the day ahead. A day that would be different to the day before and the one before that.

Life is now different.

Today we wake up in the morning in a house you can breathe in because the air is no longer tense. You can't mistake the smiles on our faces, even behind the teenage fog or hormonal flares, as the frowning brows and clenched jaws have been relegated to the past.

Life is now lighter.

Today there is space. Days are filled with meaningful work carefully selected by where my contribution can be most helpful and make the biggest impact to the business I am in. The structure of one day different to the next, because rigid routine is no longer necessary to calm my brain. Inboxes and iPhones close with the daylight, leaving an evening ahead to enjoy. I don't spend time dreading the day arriving with the next morning sun.

Life is spent learning.

Today my mind won't stop wondering, so off I go exploring, carving out time every day, to exercise my brain cells like I do my muscles. Relentlessly curious, they soak up the words from the page or the voices in my ears and connect the dots of context. They find what sparks their interest and nudge me closer, urging me to delve deeper, peel back the layers and understand more.

Life is spent serving

Today I have an overwhelming need to give back. To serve people who are lost like I was and floundering to find support. Not all of us need an MBA or a job title to be worthy of leading. Leaders don't need titles at all. Leaders know what they stand for and are committed to supporting others, to help them be the best version of themselves.

Life is spent creating

If I read something that resonates and ignites an idea, maybe I can create something that will lift another the ways others have lifted me? I put pencil to paper, never biro (pencil feels better against the page, trust me), and play with words. Words are beautiful. Their colour, their meaning, the power behind our choices. We should choose our words wisely. They have the ability to make or break someone's day.

Life is spent connecting not isolating

People continue to fascinate me. The layers of a personality formed by years of living and the art behind the process of connecting. I love asking the questions that challenge someone's thinking and listening to the stories that define their person. Emotional connection is critical to our survival. We drink when we are thirsty, eat when we are hungry. Emotional connection is the antidote to loneliness and loneliness makes us sick. I've learnt I need to resist the urge to isolate when Irene comes to visit. It would be like giving her an energy drink that would have her bouncing off the walls with sugar induced hyperactivity. Inviting someone else into my world in those moments is like a comforting hug that releases the valve.

Life is simple

My ego is no longer seduced by the designer stores on High St. Even scrolling through online shopping sites now sees me emotionally flatlined. I still like nice things, but I don't need them. I've got enough "investment pieces" to last a lifetime.

It's the simplest things that now put the biggest smile on my face.

Small gestures that leave no need to bury the mounting shame in the aftermath. The changing colour of the autumn leaves, the warmth of the afternoon sun on my skin. Teaching my kiddo to create beautiful Italian aromas in a simmering kitchen pot and watching his eyes light up with joyous love when we haven't seen each other for a week. My energy comes from things I am surrounded with that don't cost a cent. That's the price of happiness now. I can see in abundance all around me, now I have slowed down and taken the time to notice.

Life is fluid

I'm determined now to keep my brain growing, thoughts flowing and surroundings changing. To not become too fixed in my ways, galvanised in my thoughts or polarising in my perspectives. We all deserve to be able to spread our wings and explore. To not be confined to a cage wired by the perceptions of others. Diversity helps us to evolve. I've made a conscious effort for a while now to leave judgement at the door and replace it with curious exploration. We can all benefit from understanding a person or a situation a little better, even if we don't necessarily agree.

My success is no longer defined by my achievements in time. Achievements are wonderful and well deserved, but it is the lessons we learned in getting there that hold the true value.

Success is now about serving myself with the integrity I know I deserve and allowing myself the space and time to do so. Success is being kind to myself, forgiving my missteps and knowing I am enough as I am. Success is being grateful for what I have and loving every bit of my being. Success is understanding what brings me joy and making sure I commit to delivering that, every day. Success is having the confidence to go the distance.

Success is knowing the best is yet to come.

Recommended Reading
-

The Life Plan
"Simple Strategies for a Meaningful Life"
Shannah Kennedy
Published by Penguin Books (2015)

Building a Story Brand
"Clarify Your Message So Customers Will Listen"
Donald Miller
Published by Harper Collins Publishers (2017)

Eat a Peach – A Memoir
David Chang
Penguin Random House UK (2021)

The 5am Club
"Owning Your Morning, Elevate Your Life"
Robin Sharma
Published by Harper Collins Publishers (2018)

Peta Sitcheff

Good Night Irene

Epilogue

—

"It is not the critic who counts; not the man who points out how the strong man stumbles, or where the doer of deeds could have done them better. The credit belongs to the man who is actually in the arena, whose face is marred by dust, sweat and blood; who strives valiantly, who errs, who comes short again and again, because there is no effort without error and shortcoming; but who does actually strive to do the deeds; who knows great enthusiasms, the great devotions; who spends himself in a worthy cause; who at the best knows in the end the triumph of high achievement, and who at the worst, if he fails, at least fails while daring greatly, so that his place shall never be with those cold and timid souls who neither know victory or defeat."

Theodore Roosevelt

"You're just burnt out. Rest up. You'll be right"

"Nothing a few good night's sleep won't fix"

"You need a holiday"

My Beautiful Mess

"We all get stressed, it's perfectly normal"

I wasn't. It won't. It didn't help. No, it's not.

Please don't misinterpret my brevity here as dismissive or unappreciative. Without a shadow of a doubt, these comments came from a place of love embedded deep in the hearts of those in my inner sanctum. While genuineness was wrapped around the words, behind them lay a hopeless frustration provoked by a lack of awareness from yours truly. The comments slid off me like teflon, coated in oil, with a dash of salted butter.

People could have spoken to me until they were blue in the face, I wasn't listening.

My advice to my younger self:

No one can help you if you won't help yourself. It is that simple.

Your mental fitness is like your physical fitness. Be aware and work your brain like your biceps daily.

There is only one person responsible for your happiness. That is, you.

The person that is seen, is the person people come to expect.

Consider that for a moment. How would those you love, describe you?

When you ignore the desperate pleas for change from those who love you, eventually, they will stop listening. When you grind yourself to the bone, despite the protests from your own conscience, there will be consequences. When your sheer determination to live your life a certain way overrides any remaining threads of common sense screaming for change, you are playing with fire.

Peta Sitcheff

At a time when I thought I was doing my best, I now realise I was asking the impossible.

I was asking those closest to love a version of me that was very difficult to love. Heck, I didn't love her myself.

I've read many articles on burnout the past few years, "Tips to Avoid", "Know the Warning Signs", "Those most Susceptible." They all offer valid, useful advice, but within the academia, I struggled to find phrases or sentiments I could personally identify with.

By far the most powerful description I've read was summed up in five simple words:

> "Burnout is an absence of love"

An absence of love for your job.

An absence of love for your life.

An absence of love, for you.

After stumbling through the thickets of life, four years ago I hit eject. I turned my reality upside down, inside out and back the front and landed myself in a beautiful mess.

It wouldn't have mattered where I was, or what I was doing, the collision course would have been imminent until I had learnt to love the most important person in my world – me.

Today, in July 2020, like many, I find myself in a non-sensical, pandemic infested era. The ground beneath us all, has taken on a life of its own. Like an oceanic swell, it has knocked us off our foundation and tossed us

My Beautiful Mess

haphazardly in its direction of choice. I am sure I speak for many when I say, finding our feet has been a challenge, let alone determining the future direction of our compass.

I have found myself casting my mind back to four years ago. The emotional likeness to today's COVID-19 upheaval uncanny, but that is where the similarity ends. Back then, in the depths of my mess, the rest of the world was hurtling on past me at 100 mph. At the time, I felt so small in comparison. Like I was being left behind on a floating piece of driftwood in the middle of the deepest ocean.

Today, the world has slowed down with me and I find myself dancing comfortably with it through its alternating chorus. We waltz, we rap, we hip hop. As the music changes, the genres change, and I must change too.

I now recognise the beauty within those former years and the preparedness it has offered me for today.

The power of demystifying a person I never understood and the relief in welcoming another who I never knew existed.

Being trapped within the confines of my own skin with a person I didn't know let alone love, was a lonely place. It felt like there was no escape. Where I walked, she walked, where I went, she went, in a crowd of people she was there and in isolation, her presence was more intimidating than ever. I was scared of her and like a frightened child hiding behind her mother's billowy skirt, I withdrew. I wanted to run. I tried. But when I did, I couldn't shake her. I'd look over my shoulder and she was always there, never gone. A sinister, dark shadow that sucked the colour from my world and stole my ability to feel joy.

Like ominous storm clouds she would swirl overhead, reminding me that I was never in charge. I never would be, until I mustered the courage to challenge her. Until then, she would feed off my fragility, sapping my

Peta Sitcheff

confidence like a parasite feeding off its host.

Today is different because now I know. I know who she is and what she looks like.

I have given her a name.

She is no longer "the nothing" and I know, her story will not be never ending. She is very much a something, a someone who now with an identity, doesn't seem so frightening anymore.

I sat patiently in that mess, tending to each anxious knot strand by strand. Gently, untwisting and unravelling them one by one, each time freeing tension from the confines of my brain. Within the newly vacated space, I planted seeds of courage required for my new game plan.

There would be no more running and no more fighting.

It wasn't about winning or losing, it was about acceptance and the reality that like it or not, we would have to coexist.

There is and will only ever be one person leading this team and that is me.

I know what I need now and where my energy cauldrons lie. I know what I hold dearest and that the person that has emerged from the mess is actually pretty damn likeable. More than that, she is a loveable inspiration that instinctively, I feel compelled to ferociously protect with every bit of parental strength I can muster.

I threw off my armour and exposed my wounds. Putting one foot in front of the other, I paced into the messy arena and prepared myself to heal.

My scars, beautiful. *Good night Irene.*

Acknowledgements
-

It's hard to write this page without feeling emotional. Not ugly-crying emotional, like what I threw you into in Chapter One (sorry about that!). This is more relieved emotional. Proud emotional. Reflective emotional.

Shucks. You've probably worked out by now, I'm a bloody emotional person!

While I put up with me 24/7, there are those who have joined me on this wild ride who must be acknowledged. Some of you by choice (I love your madness), others by DNA (How lucky are you?!)

When I chose to take an axe to my world, I never could have predicted the mess that would ensue. It was a time that taught me the importance of not only asking for help, but for accepting the gesture of help from another.

My psychologist Jo Mitchell and her red couch at The Mind Room, was my rock. In the early days, surviving the days between sessions was a win. Each appointment breathed a bit more life into my soul. Jo, thank you for your non-judgemental ways, your compassion, and for taking me on when I know your book was full. I couldn't have done this without you.

My sister Tina Bruce, Dr Peter Larkins and Lewis's father Troy Lupoi - you were my three wise people during this time. Together, you cradled me through life and supported me with what I couldn't manage myself. The love I have for each of you is immense, my gratitude endless.

Shannah Kennedy, you tipped the first domino all those years ago. Thank you for always checking in and asking, "Am I OK?" You knew I wasn't before I did. I'm incredibly grateful for your ongoing support and now friendship.

I am incredibly lucky to be surrounded by a circle of strong, inspiring women

Peta Sitcheff

from all chapters of my life who challenge my thinking and love me for who I am. Ladies, you know who you are. Your friendships add sparkle to my life and are deeply cherished. Simply, thank you.

Vanessa Barrington, my editor from The Right Remark. Thank you for your patience in stepping this blonde rookie through the creative process. Your wisdom and encouragement fuelled my enthusiasm and brought incredible joy to the process. And to think we have done all of this via Zoom in COVID 19 lockdown, without ever properly meeting! Thank you.

Hannah Sutton, my designer. Your talent is an inspiration. You capture the nature of my brand beautifully, are a pleasure to work with and that My Beautiful Mess logo – is sublime. I feel incredibly blessed to have you on my team.

OK.

My late Dad, Eugene. While you are no longer here, the process of penning this memoir made me realise how much of you, is in me. You've given me gifts that I try to embrace every day. While some have been tricky to understand, my commitment to learning their power is relentless. I miss you.

Mum. Thea you are an inspiration. While geography separates us for now, your spirited energy crosses borders and can be felt every day. You've raised two courageous daughters, both of whom have transformed their lives in recent years and never given up. Through all you've been through, you've never given up. I love you.

My Lewis. How lucky are Dad and I to have you? Each day I marvel at your maturity and am inspired by your sensitivity towards others. You bring light and happiness to my life, a smile to my face and warmth to my heart.

I am so proud of you.

My Beautiful Mess

Peta Sitcheff